A REVIEWER WRITES...

'Would I have chosen ever to read a book on business? No.

'Would I have chosen to read a book on travel? No.

'But what a treat I would have missed if I had passed this one by.

'The first part takes the reader by road and air and foot – and occasionally by the throat and other vulnerable body parts – from São Paulo in Brazil to Venezuela, through Colombia, Ecuador, Peru and Chile, and finishes in Argentina. A travel itinerary to envy, if it were not to make routine visits to remote factories, dealing by turns with recalcitrant managers and obstructive and overly zealous security guards. Hairy moments are recounted, and the skill of the writer is that you are right there with him, sweaty and with heart palpitating as what looked simple in the planning develops regularly into anything but.

'However, all this opening is merely the set up necessary to deliver what comes next.

'In Jin-Ae, the author's female business companion for a trip to East Asia, we meet a creation of literary genius. She is a modern day, Asian Becky Sharp – and it is hard to construct a more incongruous pairing than her with her boss. Characters such as she colour life for the rest of us.

'This book is an easy, hugely enjoyable read. Don't be put off by the apparent subject matter. It is not a stodgy business manual – more a delightful, off-beat travelogue with an off-beat much travelled narrator, plenty of vivid characters to meet en route, anecdotal fun, plus an education on local cuisines. Take it as your companion read next time you travel. It will give you a lot of laughs, and the occasional cold sweat!'

Roger Ede

FORMER COLLEAGUES AND CUSTOMERS WRITE ABOUT OLIVER DOWSON

"The best part of business meetings with Oliver were listening to many of his travel stories; from interacting with Orangutans, African safaris and even the time his hotel was taken over by dissidents in India. They were never boring and a lot more interesting than any business meeting."

Reg S.

"Oliver is probably the most travelled person I know, so he is the ideal person to listen to about business travel. He truly is a 'global operator.'"

Doug Jackson

"Oliver Dowson should change his name to Oliver International. He is THE Mr International from his just-in-time travel schedule to recounting and reliving his journeys. You get an excellent imagery of the scenery and the taste and smell of the local food."

John Holding

'The most memorable parts of working with Oliver were the experiences he had on his business travels and the wealth of knowledge and understanding he had for the different Countries and their business and political cultures. He certainly got to visit some very 'different', 'remote' and sometimes 'challenging' places and cities around the world. This certainly held in good stead as he successfully set up corporate offices globally including developing countries. He was truly inspirational to work with and his appreciation of cultural diversity brought out the best in people.

NM

"Oliver has a desire for adventure and exploration. Even in the workplace. Which took him to "off the beaten track" destinations, around the globe. This gifted him a wealth of knowledge & understanding regards a vast array of business and political cultures. He shared his knowledge & experience generously, which made for a wonderful environment."

Nikki Brooker

"As somebody who makes his living helping people understand how to grow their international sales, I see Oliver Dowson as one of my few true colleagues in the field. His range of knowledge and his experience will help you navigate your way through the hardest task that faces you – expanding your global footprint"

Zach Selch

"I have known Oliver for over 20 years, in that time I have oft been regaled by his wonderful and exciting tales of travels around the globe, so what could be better than to have these stories all in one place"

Davey Johnston

"Oliver was the first executive to open the world of globalization to me when we first met during discussions for a partnership with his energy information services firm. He had constructed a service where data was collected in the US, entered into software in India, then interpreted in the UK. This enabled us to provide near real-time feedback to our clients in an unprecedented turn-around that leveraged the time zones around the globe. Subsequently, I have reached out to Oliver for insight on paths to enter new countries, and he has been informative and insightful, up to and including advising us NOT to enter certain countries. I am excited about his book and will among the first to buy and share with my colleagues."

Ralph F. Tschantz

ABOUT THE AUTHOR

OLIVER DOWSON spent a long career building a small multi-national business from scratch, exploiting his love of foreign travel, cultures, languages and food. He has visited over 140 countries for business and pleasure – and tries to add at least one new one every year! Oliver also hosts the Grow Through International Expansion podcast, website and app, writes many articles, and mentors and supports several new young ambitious entrepreneurs. He lives between North London and Asturias, Spain – when he's not away adding new countries and experiences further afield.

THERE'S NO BUSINESS LIKE INTERNATIONAL BUSINESS

FACED WITH BLAZING BUSES IN VENEZUELA...
TERRIFYING FLIGHTS IN ECUADOR AND ARGENTINA...
SCREAMING MATCHES IN THE STREET IN SHANGHAI AND SEOUL...
JUST ANOTHER BUSINESS TRIP... ALL IN THE PURSUIT OF... WHAT?

OLIVER DOWSON

Matador
Unit E2 Airfield Business Park,
Harrison Road, Market Harborough,
Leicestershire. LE16 7UL
Tel: 0116 2792299
Email: books@troubador.co.uk
Web: www.troubador.co.uk/matador
Twitter: @matadorbooks

ISBN 978 1803131 917

British Library Cataloguing in Publication Data.
A catalogue record for this book is available from the British Library.

Printed and bound in Great Britain by 4edge Limited
Typeset in 11pt Minion Pro by Troubador Publishing Ltd, Leicester, UK

Matador is an imprint of Troubador Publishing Ltd

For all my former colleagues in offices around the world,
who patiently tolerated me, listened to my stories,
and laughed in all the right places – and especially
those who told me "you should write a book
about your travels some day".

CONTENTS

PART ONE

A SOUTH AMERICAN BUSINESS ODYSSEY

PART TWO

A FAR EASTERN BUSINESS ODYSSEY

ARRIVAL

It's nearly nightfall. I am at the wheel of a rental car that I picked up just five minutes ago at São Paulo airport. The car, a Fiat Punto, seems fairly new, but is very basic, and extremely noisy. The controls are on the opposite side of the wheel to the car I'm used to. It's uncomfortable too, and I'm irritated, already thinking I was foolish to refuse to pay the 20 *reais* a day supplement for a better car. Foolish to rent a car at all, since I've already been travelling for sixteen hours. But here I am.

I am trying to get to an airport hotel. I can see it. I know it's the right hotel because the name is shining out from the top of it in 10-foot-high illuminated letters. It is huge. It is right next to the highway. But there is no exit. I have no idea how to get there or, more pressingly, how to get off this road in the first place. There's a lot of traffic and, worse, motorcycles with no lights are buzzing past me on the nearside. They all know where they are going and are determined to go there as fast as they can. They have no patience for a foreign visitor searching for an exit. This is no time to learn to drive all over again.

Seeing a pillion passenger on the bike in front of me twist towards me (fortunately just to adjust his or her jacket), I'm reminded of the news article from the Chicago Tribune that an American colleague sent me a week or so ago. All about drive-by shootings in São Paulo. I'd dismissed it as I figured it was a journalist exaggerating and trying to shift the issue away from his home city. I try not to get any more nervous.

Eventually, perhaps 5km further on, there's an exit. By then, I've left the hotel far behind, the traffic has become paralysed, and I have been crawling along for what feels like hours, but was probably ten minutes, in the slow lane of a wide and extraordinarily busy highway headed, I think, for the city centre. I'm not certain, because there have been no signs – well, no helpful ones – but, now night has fallen, there's a glow on the horizon that is I am sure is getting brighter.

At last, there's an exit. A roundabout. Two roads leading off that, neither of them signed to anywhere. Take a chance on the one that looks like it's sort of headed back to where I've come from.

At first, the feeling of relief at leaving the motorway and reaching a quiet road. Then, minor panic. This road is *very* quiet. Dead, in fact. There are no streetlights. No other cars. No signs. But then, suddenly, I see lights approaching – and I realise I am on the wrong side of the road.

But to every cloud, a silver lining. The oncoming van stops, the driver gets out to remonstrate with me – but, instantly registering that I'm a foreigner, and with me jabbering away about the hotel name, he cheerily points to the other exit off the roundabout – that road looks even more minor – high-fives me and goes on his way.

Thirty minutes and a few more wrong turns later, I'm in the hotel. Frazzled, ready for a shower and desperate for a long sleep. I need to be bright-eyed in the morning. Ready for my mission. Ready for business.

INTRODUCTION

Before we go any further, I need to give you some background. This book is in two parts; each a story about a long business trip that I made, the first around South America, the second around East Asia.

This is not a business book, nor a how-to guide. Indeed, if you, the reader, are ever called on to make a trip for a similar purpose, you might only acquire here tips on how *not* to do it.

It's not an autobiography. It only covers around five weeks of my life. There are no insights into my childhood or anything like that.

Rather, it's 'factual fiction', a travelogue interlaced with asides about my loves of food and travel. Some contemporaries (who happen to be old enough to know) have compared me to Ronnie Corbett for my tendency to deviate; if, as you read, you wonder if I've forgotten I'm telling a story, stay with me, the plot will resume a few pages later.

These trips are not typical of the journeys most business travellers make. In fact, they're quite unusual, both in their purpose and planning.

In the 20 years since I made these journeys, lots of things have changed, but most significantly, the smartphone hadn't been invented. So, no Google Maps, no Flightstats, no WhatsApp, no Zoom, no built-in camera – you get the picture. Or not, as it happens!

Although I didn't keep a diary, almost every detail of these trips leaps to mind as if they had taken place only a few months ago. Every significant event in the book actually happened. However, I can't pretend that all the smaller details and dialogue are fully accurate recollections; so let's allow some artistic licence...

All the characters also are real, though their names have, of course, been changed. I genuinely liked everyone I've written about, even the ones who drove me to drink or desperation, so I can guarantee nothing is libellous.

So, if you think you know what happens on business trips abroad, well, you might be right about a lot of them. But not all of them. Read this book and think again.

BUSINESS TRIPS
AND WHY I LOVE THEM

Lots of people complain they hate overseas business trips. Some will tell you they hate the travel itself, or they hate staying in hotels, or they hate the food. Many worry about a language barrier. Some are uncomfortable having business dinners with overseas customers or colleagues; they might not want to be sociable, or they may be reluctant to pretend to like local delicacies, or they might genuinely have enforced or chosen selective diets. Although the company's paying, some even say they hate having to file expense reports. Many more simply just don't want to be away from their partner and family and their normal routines.

I'm not like them. I adore business travel just as much as holiday travel.

Firstly, it's the perfect excuse for getting out of the office.

I love going to fresh places, exploring, and meeting new people; equally, I love returning to familiar places and faces. Above all else, I believe the fundamental reasons behind every business trip should be to discover facts and meet people face to face, to spend time with them, to start to understand the way they think, and try to build a relationship. Whether you're selling, consulting, training, or just box-ticking, simply 'being there' and 'being with the people' achieves results that even the most effective applications of video-conferencing cannot.

I love every aspect of the experience – the travel itself, just as much as the meetings and visits. When it all goes to plan, I love the satisfaction of a trip well organised and a job well done. When little things go wrong, I love rearranging meetings and flights and hotels and whatever on the fly. When *big* things go wrong, my stress levels go up like everyone else's but, when I look back afterwards, I realise I loved the frisson, the excitement, and having lived through – and resolved – a crisis.

I've been lucky. I was the boss. I could make my own plans, choose my own flights and hotels, and do what I wanted; well, within the confines of what made business sense and what the company could afford. I couldn't afford to fly first class, or stay in real luxury hotels, even if I'd wanted to, especially in the early years. Being a business owner makes one far more cost-conscious, to the extent of only travelling when one can be sure that the value will exceed the expense, and then looking to cut that cost wherever it's reasonably possible.

I've always seen travel as a privilege and an opportunity, and I've never understood why so many moan, rather than appreciating that they're actually being paid to have the opportunity of seeing other places and meeting other people. You, the reader, will have your own opinion!

Most business travellers miss out on a lot of the enjoyment, and end up with less desirable itineraries and experiences, simply because they don't plan the trip themselves. Executives leave it to their PAs, lower rungs leave it to the company travel department, and in most cases, both of those pass it all on to a travel agent, whose interpretation of their standing instructions is to book the most obvious option at the highest price the company travel policy will allow.

That's not for me. I love booking flights – researching alternatives, looking for the best connections, working out how and where to get the lowest prices. Now, with the internet, it's very easy, and accessible to all. Travel agents are unnecessary. But when I worked as one, for a year or two in the 1970s, travel agents were needed and, unless it was just a matter of booking a package holiday out of a brochure, they needed some expertise. I specialised then in booking complicated round-the-world itineraries for others, and dreamt of the day when I could plan such journeys for myself. Having caught the passion, making reservations has never since been anything I could leave to others.

But that is as nothing compared to the travel itself.

Once on the plane, I love sitting in a window seat and watching the world far beneath me, feeling the intense privilege and joy of being able to travel. I love listening to the changing sounds of the engines and wing flaps, instinctively knowing when we're climbing and descending (and when something sounds wrong!). On longer flights, I love the inflight service – nothing cheers like a glass or two of champagne at 39,000 feet!

When I'm not looking out of the window, drinking, eating or sleeping, I can work – and that's generally undisturbed and can be unbelievably productive.

Once I've arrived, I love the sights and the sounds, whether the place is new to me or a frequent destination. But, above all, I love the people – all people, all nationalities. That's where business travel really comes into its own. Tourists may meet hotel receptionists, waiters, taxi drivers, tour guides, but they might rarely have conversations with them. A tourist may watch locals and have fleeting interactions with them, but not get to know them ever.

Business travel, however, by definition, involves meeting and conversing with local people. Salespeople meet customers, buyers meet salespeople, engineers meet other engineers, and so on.

The most important lesson I have learnt through all my business travelling is that people are wonderful and interesting, the world over. 99.9% of people, regardless of race, religion, country, age or anything else, simply want to have the best and happiest life that they can, and try to make the world a better place, so that their children and grandchildren can enjoy an even better and happier life than theirs. And almost everyone enjoys meeting and conversing with people from another country.

During the Coronavirus pandemic there were many places which were mandated as off limits even for 'essential' business trips. Some other countries or cities may feel too risky even in normal times. There's always tests, forms and hassle, whatever you do and wherever you go. The attraction of new technology is obvious; so much international business can now be done by Zoom, Microsoft Teams,

Skype and other conferencing tools. That said, it would be a terrible mistake to stop travelling altogether. A remote video business meeting is a sterile thing, existing purely for its specific purpose. One can never get to know the people properly; there's no opportunity to watch body language, see the nuances of facial expression, no chit-chat, no meals together.

Of course, there's a routine element to every trip. Writing up the day's notes, determining which scraps of paper to keep and which to bin. Late evening and early morning calls and emails to catch up with family, office and customers. The engineering feat of making showers work in strange bathrooms and keeping power adaptors connected. Fear not, I don't intend to bore you with any of that.

The trips I'll tell you about were definitely worthwhile and necessary; I couldn't have done them by Zoom, even if it had existed then. What came out of these little odysseys created and maintained worthwhile and well-paid work for dozens of people in many countries, in many cases leading to satisfying careers.

PART ONE

A SOUTH AMERICAN BUSINESS ODYSSEY

INTRODUCTION

Early November, 2002. I don't remember the reasons why I decided to pack nine business visits, each taking most of a day, each in different cities, across seven countries of South America, into just a fortnight. I was younger. I probably had a deadline, and I would not have wanted to be away from the office for too long. But I must have been more than a little crazy to do it in such a short timespan, and certainly very conceited in advance about my travel planning abilities.

For many years, my company had been successfully selling data processing services to big multi-nationals, ones with branches and offices and factories in many countries. When I say data, I mean energy and water bills. At first, we'd only worked on data for the client's home country, in most cases the UK or USA. As we got better at what we did, and our customers got more committed to our services, we'd faced a combination of opportunity and demand to expand what we were doing to their facilities in other countries around the world. Being salespeople, our response was always "of course we can do that".

But selling is one thing, delivering is another.

The reality hit home when thousands of documents started to arrive that we couldn't process. Languages nobody in the company understood. Numbers on the bills that made no sense. Either we admitted defeat, and risked losing all the business we'd worked for years to build up, or we solved the problem. One way was to learn about the source of the numbers on the bills at first hand, by going to some of the sites. Another was to construct an international operation, hiring staff with the necessary language and cultural skills. We needed to do both. I had to start making more business trips to more countries…

South America

VALENCIA CARACAS
BOGOTA
QUITO
LIMA
TACNA
ARICA
SAO PAULO
ROSARIO
SANTIAGO
BUENOS AIRES

WEEK 1 - DAY 1
BRAZIL; START AS YOU MEAN TO GO ON

Suitably refreshed after a long sleep, my somewhat traumatic and unnecessarily long drive from the airport to the hotel the previous night now forgotten, I got back into my rental car on Monday morning looking forward to my first business day in Brazil.

Why, you might ask, was I driving myself? Why not get a taxi? Two reasons: previous experience and excessive over-confidence. The former happened the year before, when I'd made an initial exploratory visit to one of the factories – the one that I was going to go to the next day. It was in a suburb of São Paulo, perhaps 20km from the centre. It had been easy to get a taxi there from my hotel; the driver was no doubt happy with the high fare. Had I known how long I'd be at the plant, I might have asked him to wait, or at least have inquired about getting back – but I didn't. Since the streets around the factory seemed full of taxis, I'd anticipated no problem.

I had ended up in meetings of one kind or another for most of the day, and only got to leave the factory when my host was going home himself. It had been a good day, and I'd left feeling satisfied. But then I'd started looking for a taxi.

Now it was rush hour, and all the ones that passed me were full. At the end of the road I found a taxi rank and joined a queue; however, when my turn came, the driver refused to go to São Paulo city. So did the next. And the next. There were plenty of people on the street, but nobody either spoke English or could understand my Spanish, which I'd wrongly assumed was similar enough to Portuguese and so would get me understood. Not the case.

Eventually – I suppose it was ten minutes, but it felt like hours – I found someone who spoke English and explained to me this was technically a different city, and local taxis were not allowed to drive into São Paulo itself; I would either have to find an SP taxi that was returning empty, or phone for one to come and pick me up.

Easier to catch a bus, I thought. Lots of those – but every one of them packed to the gills. It's difficult to work out what bus to catch in SP even today; there are hundreds of routes, operated by dozens of different companies, with no route map or even a plate on the bus stop to show what routes stop there and where they go on to. No doubt there's now an app for that, but there weren't any smartphones then. The destination names were on placards in the front window of the bus, but they're the names of squares, streets, markets and so on, that locals know, but foreigners don't. And it would probably have taken me longer to find them on a street map of São Paulo than to walk all the way.

So, putting my faith in other passengers who told me it was definitely going to the city, I boarded a bus and spent well over an hour standing, swaying and trying to look out of the window to guess where we were. Traffic was solid, as expected. When we moved, we crawled. Eventually the bus reached somewhere that seemed significant – at least, somewhere a lot of people were getting off – and, sure enough, I was in the city, and there were taxis. The wrong side of the city, as it transpired, so a long taxi ride ensued. Nearly four hours from leaving the factory to reaching the hotel. I wasn't doing that again.

Thus, on the basis that I'd rented and driven cars in many other countries, find driving on the right as natural as driving on the left, that the taxi journey to the factory had seemed straightforward enough, and that I had three other factories to visit in Brazil, all in the region though a little further afield, it seemed a natural decision to rent a car for this trip and drive myself. Total flexibility. No problems. *Ha.*

Driving is one thing. Navigating is another. These days we have smartphones with Google Maps and dozens of other satnav apps. Even in strange countries on the other side of the world, one can never get badly lost. Back then, though, with no apps, no satnav, and not much in the way of mobile phone coverage, it was very different. Very easy to get lost.

I did have one of those old-fashioned printed maps, though – indeed, it proved to be quite a good one (once I'd got the hang of how it was marked up), so good in fact that I carried on using it for another 15 years. On its first outings, however, I often felt it only made things more confusing.

And it was a big folded-up single sheet; not very practical for checking while driving.

So, to help me follow the best route to my first destination on the Monday morning, I'd printed out a map with turn-by-turn directions using what was then a very popular online web tool: MapQuest. I'd already been relying on it for several years driving round the USA. The fact that they 'covered' Brazil had added to the little encouragement I'd needed to rent a car and drive myself.

It didn't take me very long to discover MapQuest's limitations when it came to Brazil. The map itself was accurate, in that south was south and north was north, and the start and end points were indeed where one wanted to begin and finish. The roads in between probably did all exist. But some of the turnings didn't seem to be there, or had 'no entry' signs and, even when they were where they were supposed to be, the signs pointed to the names of places that I couldn't find on the map at all.

A not-insubstantial further difficulty was that I'd chosen to travel to my first factory in the São Paulo morning rush hour, and that the route involved crossing the city centre. In those days – and still now to some extent – the rush hour basically meant stationary traffic. The chief topic of the traffic news on the radio, insofar as I could understand it, was whether the cumulative total of traffic jams across the city was increasing or reducing – the number seemed to range up and down from 200km.

Only the cars and trucks were standing still, though. Brave locals who wanted to travel quickly rode motorbikes, zipping between lanes of cars and trucks, just millimetres away. Dangerous for them – I've now seen dozens of bike accidents in and around São Paulo – and frightening for car drivers as, when looking in the rear-view mirror, it's hard to predict whether a bike will pass on the right or the left, making it extremely difficult to change lanes safely (on the rare occasions that there's a gap to move into).

These were not narrow roads. They were highways, with up to six lanes in each direction – and, in one case, with a parallel set of six-line highways, thus totalling twelve lanes each way. To this day, although many improvements have speeded up the traffic, that parallel road situation creates peril for any inexperienced driver or cautious foreigner. The inner highway is the 'express' road, and it's only possible to exit to another road from the parallel 'local' highway. If you find yourself on the 'express', and you have an exit coming up – maybe 5km ahead – you'll need to move onto the 'local', but that's only possible once every few kilometres. If you don't move over soon enough, you find yourself trapped. Missing your exit, taking the next one from the express lane and then the next on the local may easily mean that you've gone nearly 10km past where you wanted to be. Worse still, there are no lay-bys or parking places to stop along the road – and, even if one could, back in 2002, when mobile data didn't exist, there was no way to log into MapQuest and print out new directions. Thank goodness for the occasional petrol station, the only opportunity where one could stop to study the map and ask directions.

The other distraction is helicopters. The occasional one, perhaps monitoring traffic, isn't unusual anywhere. But in the skies over São Paulo there are a lot; maybe not a swarm, as such, but enough to take one's eye off the stationary traffic queue ahead until blaring horns from behind return one to reality. The rich, rather than spending their gains on taxes that might get more roads and rails built, instead buy themselves helicopters to travel to and from the office, with many skyscrapers boasting a helipad on the roof.

In the end, I made it. The journey, with all its missed exits, wrong turns and stationary traffic, gave me an unplanned opportunity of seeing a lot of the São Paulo urban sprawl, confirming in my mind that it's not ever likely to become a number one tourist destination. On the whole, it's an ugly city. My drive included a few neighbourhoods that I instantly decided I should get out of fast and never return. In one I was stopped by traffic police at a junction where they had six men lying down on the road in front of me, with other officers pointing guns at them.

I learnt a lot about driving in Brazil in just that single two-hour journey. I realised that when behind the wheel, caution and good manners needed to be forgotten. Motorbikes appear from nowhere. Making space for ambulances to squeeze past and keeping one's car scratch-free are incompatible. That old age and poor maintenance make buses and trucks belch choking fumes, and rental cars aren't fitted with gas masks. That vehicles of all kinds, large and small, overheat and break down with monotonous frequency, trapping queues of traffic behind them, the solid nose-to-tail traffic of adjacent lanes making it impossible to escape. I learnt that you'll never go hungry or thirsty or without a phone charging cable, as a motley mafia of roadside vendors, young, old, male and female, materialise at hundred metre intervals whenever traffic is paralysed which, as you've gathered, is most of the time.

The journey should have taken 45 minutes rather than two hours, of course, but I contented myself with thinking that it was still quicker than my previous four-hour experience, and that I'd do it better next time.

During the journey, I also worked out that the reason the signposts are unhelpful to foreigners is that they don't usually show the name of the city or town or suburb that the road leads to. They put the name of the road instead. In Brazil, every road, bridge and viaduct has been given a name, usually that of some long-forgotten personage who was once famous for doing something worthy, also long-forgotten. Honestly, every one of them; on later treks, deeper into the country, I've even found unsurfaced dirt tracks given names. I'm never likely to have even five minutes of fame, but if I did, I don't think I'd want to be remembered by a dirt track going from Nowhere Town to Obscure Village.

So, even though there are two more or less parallel motorways going there from São Paulo, you can search in vain for a signpost to Rio de Janeiro. Instead, you need to look for signs either for Dutra (having read Wikipedia, I learn historians consider him one of Brazil's better 20th century presidents) or Ayrton Senna (the motor racing legend). Oh, and if you join a road part way along, you'll need to know if you want to go east, west, north or south. Not always obvious, I discovered, as on a very bendy road, even if you want to go east, the road might be going north at that point. Just forget the name of the place you're looking for until the final exit, when it might at last appear on a sign.

The journey completed and forgotten, my day at the factory proved satisfying. As I already had a good contact,

I didn't need to find someone to be supportive and help find the bills. There was already an enthusiasm for energy management and, indeed, an unusual sense of urgency about it. As there needed to be, because there were acute energy shortages in Brazil at that time. Every business was being legally obliged to cut its electricity consumption by 15%, with the threat that if it didn't, the government would shut down the power to their site completely.

That wasn't down to environmental activism, but was an early indirect result of global warming. Brazil gets about 90% of its electricity from hydro – and, in the year before my visit, it had hardly rained. That meant the rivers and reservoirs were running dry, leading to an acute shortage of electricity. Despite that, the factory was working and at full production – but very much in the dark. It is strange to be wandering around a busy factory in the gloaming, light only coming from a few roof windows.

They hadn't turned off the lights only to save electricity – they'd come up with dozens of original ideas. By the time of this trip, I'd already been working in energy management with big corporations for just over 20 years, during which the motivation for saving energy had changed several times. When I'd begun, the issue was 'saving the planet'. This did not involve ecological concerns about greenhouse gases – other than acknowledging the risk to the ozone layer, the dominant implication was always that it was too far away to worry about, so they hardly got a mention. But in the early 1980s, with coal already on its way out, there was genuine concern that there were only sufficient recoverable fossil fuels – oil, gas and uranium – left in the ground to last perhaps 25 years. Had the dire warnings in the books I'd read then come true, we would all by now be relying on tallow candles for light and wearing animal skins to keep warm!

But the oil companies kept drilling and finding more reserves, so within a few years, those worries went out of the window. The emphasis then moved on to the more universal and certainly more marketable philosophy of saving money by reducing waste. Energy management basically meant switching things off when not needed, although we always made it sound a lot more scientific than that.

More recently, in the late 1990s, as competitive private electricity and gas suppliers began to proliferate, the emphasis shifted again, particularly in the UK, USA and Australia, this time simply to buying energy more cheaply. Now all we had to do was negotiate lower prices. There was plenty of scope; while energy companies were state monopolies, governments had deliberately pushed up the price of energy over previous years to 'fatten up' the industry for privatisation. In fact, the price of electricity and gas paid by industry and commerce then dropped so much that retrofit measures to reduce energy usage, such as insulation, more efficient equipment, and controls to switch things off automatically, all became uneconomic overnight. Purists like me, early embracers of the 'save it' philosophy, were saddened that nobody seemed to care anymore. However, pragmatism ruled: while nobody wanted engineering advice to find ways of reducing their energy usage any longer, the new demand for professional services to negotiate lower prices in the newly competitive energy market was very good for business. So, we evolved.

A few years later, having got as much blood out of one stone as was possible, and with dire warnings of global warming now appearing in the news every day, the emphasis changed again, this time to reducing a company's carbon footprint. Burning electricity, gas and oil generates carbon dioxide, tons and tons of it, and so we simply moved the focus from measuring energy and cost to measuring CO_2 emissions. But that stage hadn't been reached by the time of this South American visit.

Not that any of that mattered; regardless of the motivation, we were still doing the same thing – helping measure and save energy. However, despite all our client companies believing and talking the talk, very few of them were doing anything serious about it.

This factory, like all the ones that I was to visit over the coming two weeks, built cars. It belonged to our biggest client, an American company, and they were very serious about saving energy. The system that we'd developed had been working well for them in the USA for a couple of years, but their plants (their name for factories) in that home country only accounted for about half their global energy usage. It was time to be brave, and roll out the system across the world.

For me, visiting a factory where they were actively and willingly trying hard to reduce their energy usage significantly was quite exciting! They were doing lots of little things – as simple as switching off lights and machines not in use. The staff did it manually. Obvious of course. Not like back home, where no shop-floor human would take responsibility, and all the switches stayed on until the company employed a dedicated and trained turner-offer, or invested in automatic controls. What struck me most, though, was that they'd taken a decision to paint all the cars the same colour; silver. I learnt that switching paint colours through the day wastes a lot of energy. They'd also turned this energy-saving initiative into a public relations triumph; they were promoting it in their advertising as a 'Silver Anniversary Celebration'.

My mission, though, was not to celebrate their splendid efforts or longevity, but to get hold of those energy bills. Just as importantly, I needed to identify exactly what each bill related to.

In a new factory, even a very big one, there's usually only one electricity, gas and water supply, so just three bills every month. This, however, was an old factory, started in 1930, and expanded massively over the next 70 years through acquisition of adjacent land and buildings. Every addition meant more meters and more bills. By now, there were at least 20 monthly electricity bills for different buildings and zones. Some had easy-to-understand supply addresses, but others had unhelpful identifiers like 'zone 32', and sometimes nothing at all. Without going and looking, nobody could work what bill related to what.

Understanding what all the bills related to meant walking round the entire site – about two kilometres from one end to the other – with a helpful maintenance manager, my new friend, Nelson. Yes, named after the famous sea lord. Lots of Brazilians have names like Nelson, Wilson, Washington, Wagner and Wellington; the consensus among those who have studied the origins is that Brazilians are besotted with celebrity and believe that giving their boys names like these will help advance them in life. They're always male, by the way; I've never come across any girls named after famous women. The theory also goes that this is something done by the lower classes, but there are many successful businessmen and politicians with that kind of name. Maybe they were all born poor and the name worked for them, but I doubt it.

In being teamed with Nelson, I was doubly lucky. Firstly, he was genuinely willing to help, take the time and make the required effort. Secondly, Nelson actually knew the factory like the back of his own hand and could identify most of the meters, not that that held him back from stopping to ask advice and opinions from others along the way. Even though he'd been working there for many years, our tour yielded additional facts he'd never known before, and he got more excited with every new discovery.

Lunch time couldn't come fast enough for him to tell his friends and colleagues all about our morning's adventure. We ate in a vast canteen, where Nelson presided over a rare window table with, as best as I could gather, his entire team of site engineers and mechanics. He was obviously well-liked, and it impressed me how effectively he spread his enthusiasm for hitherto-lost meters, dodgy cabling, leaking steam pipes and deficient insulation to a bunch of guys who, from first impressions, I'd have thought would have much preferred to have been discussing football. Rafael, who I was told was the newest team member, having only started the week before, started shovelling his meal in as fast as he could so that not a minute would be wasted before he could go and turn off a pump and stick some new warning signs in a remote outbuilding nobody had apparently visited in years. I've never seen anyone look so happy to be getting back to work.

After everyone else had left, I did get a few quiet minutes with Nelson and a *cafezinho* to chat about something not related to energy. Like me, he was an enthusiastic home cook, and especially passionate about Italian food. Indeed, he claimed to be Italian, at least by descent. We were of one mind on pizzas. However, once we got onto the subject of making pasta at home by hand, something which I thought was an unnecessary waste of time, he quickly moved to avert an argument by reminding me that we had better get back to the mission.

By late afternoon, I'd accumulated a fat file of bills, extensive scrawled explanatory notes, a promise from Nelson that he'd make sure that we got all the bills and information we wanted every month for ever and ever thereafter, and near total exhaustion. Memo to self: don't commit to spending a whole day on your feet trying to understand a complex set of information delivered in another language without first getting fitter and learning a bit more Portuguese.

But, as with so many lessons like that, it was too late for this trip. I knew I'd have to do it all again the next day, and for more days after that.

Having bid farewell to my very helpful new friend, I headed back to my car. Silver! I'd not registered the colour before. Perhaps Fiat were doing the same thing. I slumped into the driver's seat, and reached for my MapQuest route back to the hotel. OK, I thought, this looks straightforward enough. But no. The very first turn was prohibited, and the road, after enough bends to disorientate me, then ended at a T-junction with a completely different highway to the one I was expecting, with a name I didn't recognise, obscure even in a pantheon of obscurity. I knew that I needed to go roughly north, but the choice was east or west. And I was now hitting the evening rush hour. Two hours later...

Showered, I logged in and trawled the day's emails. Nothing that couldn't wait; I needed dinner. Specifically, feeling exceptionally carnivorous, I needed *picanha* and a *cerveja bem gelada*. The hotel restaurant looked quite nice, but couldn't meet that need; the maître d' recommended a *churrascaria*. Frankly, I didn't much feel like getting back in the car and risking getting lost at night again, but he assured me that it was only five minutes away, and that I couldn't go wrong. Brazilian cuisine deserves a chapter to itself, so if you don't know what *picanha* or *cerveja bem gelada* is, I'll enlighten you in a few pages' time.

WEEK 1 - DAY 2
INTO THE FIERY FURNACE

I awoke as bright as the morning sun, totally looking forward to my next car factory adventure. Indiana Jones, you have no idea how exciting life can really be. Forget Lost Arks. Hunt down electricity bills!

I'd slept like the proverbial log. Fortunately, one suffers very little jetlag when flying to Brazil – the time difference is only two or three hours. It's just a very long flight, but usually all in daylight. As a result, my slumber resulted merely from exhaustion and, most likely though I don't precisely recall, a medicinal dose of alcohol either in celebration for making it back to the hotel, or to calm the accumulated stress – or both.

The next plant I was going to visit was about 100km east of the city – a simple journey along a single motorway, Dutra, driving in the opposite direction to the main traffic flow, or so I hoped.

That didn't mean an empty road, as there's never a time when the motorways are quiet in Brazil. Any of them, in any direction, any hour, day or night. There's a never-ending procession of trucks in various stages of antiquity. Perhaps most are not actually overloaded; but if that's not the reason for the constant belching of black exhaust fumes, then old age and lack of maintenance must be to blame.

I quickly learnt that getting stuck behind one or more of them on a hill was a real danger to health. Turning off the ventilation fan did no good; the fumes found their way in anyway, and the dirt belched out from the lorry in front clouded the windscreen within minutes. I also realised that while rental cars have screen washers, they don't put any detergent in the water, and so using them just turns dense murk into zero visibility and the inability to discern anything ahead at all. Another lesson learned; stop at the first gas station after renting a car and buy a bottle of screen wash fluid! And a cleaning cloth!

On this drive, the traffic didn't prove too much of a hindrance, and getting to the factory was quick enough. I could even see it from the motorway. Like many huge car plants, though, actually getting into it wasn't so simple. These factories always have lots of entrance gates and, needless to say, I started at the wrong one. Anyway, third time lucky; yes, they had numbers, but the signage wasn't very obvious, and I only saw where the gate numbers were positioned once I reached the third one. By then, it felt like the drive around the plant perimeter had taken longer than the drive from my hotel.

There was a real 'jobsworth' on Security. Lucky me. Whether he was always like that, got out of bed on the wrong side that morning, or was just prejudiced against foreigners,

I'll never know, but I remember everything taking ages and very nearly losing my temper.

It started with the parking. I knew I wouldn't be allowed to drive into the plant. Conveniently, though, there was a visitors' car park right in front of the gate, marked out into ten bays, and with precisely zero other cars parked there. I parked neatly in the first bay, got out, and locked the doors. I then heard someone shouting at me – the security guard. He raced out of his hut towards me, gesticulating wildly. I couldn't understand a word he was saying, but it seemed pretty obvious that it meant "you can't park here". He pointed to the bottom of the hill.

OK, no point in arguing. I drove down the hill to where I saw some other cars parked and pulled up there. I climbed the hill back to the hut, no longer in the best of moods.

Nor, when I reached the hut, was the guard. He wouldn't call Roberto, the guy I was going to meet, until I'd first filled in a long form. I'd never had to do that at any of the other plants I'd visited, even though they were part of the same company. He then made me remove everything from my briefcase (we still had them in those days). He didn't like my ID – I'd left my passport behind in the hotel, so I gave him my driving licence, hoping it looked official enough. He could or would only speak Portuguese, and made a meal of trying to understand my Spanish. However, he did understand the words 'driving licence'. Whether they were the only English words he understood or was prepared to understand, it didn't matter – he didn't like it. He kept turning my little plastic card over and over and round and round, regularly tapping with his forefinger at the words 'driving licence'. No idea why. Perhaps he was hoping it would turn into some other sort of ID card he recognised. Maybe he was trying to cast a spell to make me disappear.

He was also super-suspicious of my laptop. Roberto, when I was finally allowed to meet him, told me that he probably just didn't believe it was a computer because it was so small, less than half the size of the electronic bricks they used in the factory.

In the end, of course, I made it through; but it had taken more than an hour from the time I arrived at the first gate to finally passing the security tests and being allowed in. Now I had to wait for Roberto to come and get me. Fortunately, his office was near the gate, but in a Portakabin far distant from everything else on the site. I'd thought the plant yesterday was big, but this one seemed seriously enormous.

"Why wouldn't he let me park by the gate?" I asked Roberto. "It says 'Visitors.'"

"You're driving the wrong brand of car. He's only allowed to have our own cars park there."

That explained that. Memo to self: next time I rent a car, get the right kind.

Before doing anything else, I needed to see those bills. For most of the plants I was visiting, they had already sent me images of at least a few of the bills by email, so I'd got some idea of what to expect, but I had nothing for this place. I'd hoped that Roberto would have got them ready, but I learned that all he'd done was call a friend in Accounts to prepare them for me, and we'd have to walk over there first. "Over there" was in fact about a kilometre away, an office building that, ironically, was right next to the very first factory gate I'd arrived at and been sent away from.

I knew that this was their biggest factory in Brazil but, even after the long drive around the perimeter to find the right gate, I only now started to appreciate the scale. Not that it was architecturally impressive; it was just a lot of huge grey sheds interspersed with smaller huts, roads, parking lots, and so on. All shades of grey; possibly fifty, I wasn't counting. Roberto's English was enough to communicate, but he didn't want to chat. Perhaps he just wasn't much of a conversationalist, as he wasn't willing to engage with my attempts in Spanish either.

But along the way, he did at least try to explain what was what and where. 'Press shop', pointing in one direction. 'Final assembly', pointing to another. 'Paint shop', pointing towards a third. They all looked the same to me.

"I need to get the bills first," I told him. "Then we can go back and look."

"That one is different," he said, as we passed yet another grey shed. "Foundry. Only one we have in South America."

It piqued my interest. I'd never been to a foundry. "Can we go in?" I asked.

"Yes, but don't go near the furnaces. You'll see why." About the most Roberto had said since we left the guardhouse.

The shed might have looked like a modern grey warehouse from the outside, but inside, to me, it looked like a scene from Dante's Inferno. It was obvious where a lot, if not most, of the energy used by the factory was going – into boiling iron and aluminium in huge vats. Teams of men, encrusted with grime and streaming in sweat, toiled at the furnaces, pouring the molten metal into moulds to make engine blocks. Now I understood why Roberto had advised me not to go near. Even standing by the wide-open doors, I was already sweating profusely and, lacking a mask, was covering my mouth and nose with a handkerchief. The sight was fascinating and encouraged me to get closer; but I wasn't dressed for the part, nor there to learn about industrial processes. Back to reality. And energy bills.

Roberto seemed to have rather a lot of friends in Accounts – by the time he'd greeted and chatted with most of them, it was getting near to lunch time. It became quickly obvious that this was the most important part of the day for Roberto. So, with a folder stuffed with bills under my arm, we headed for the cafeteria, my companion enthusiastically telling me how good the food was. What gourmet delights awaited?

On which note, permit me to deviate from my story for just a few pages and tell you about Brazilian food.

A SIDE NOTE ON MY LOVE OF BRAZILIAN FOOD

One has only to look around in the street to know that the diet of most Brazilians isn't good for the health. There seem to be a huge number of overweight and obese people. From my observations, an awful lot of Brazilians display non-existent fashion sense, and a surprisingly large number of them choose to wear figure-hugging leggings and tops in garish, clashing colours. There's no hiding place for excess body fat dressed like that.

Even at its best, I don't imagine that Brazilian food will ever get top marks from gourmets, and the national diet, insofar as there is one, will never gain the kudos of the Mediterranean one. But that doesn't mean there's not good – and original – food to enjoy. I love eating in Brazil.

The day starts with breakfast. In hotels, it's included in the rate by even the most upmarket and poshest establishments. Sharing the buffet with Brazilians travelling on business and watching their choices is a great indication of their attitude towards diet. There's fabulous tropical fruit trays; papaya, pineapple, passion fruit… that the locals all seem to avoid. Instead, they head straight for the *petiscos* – small fried snacks. There can be a wide variety of these little delicacies, though arrive late for the buffet and you'll certainly find all the good ones gone.

You won't find the best *petiscos* on a hotel breakfast buffet, though. Get a local to recommend a *padaria* (bakery) to buy *cozinhas* – essentially a large stuffed croquette, thick bechamel wrapped around a filling, most commonly of minced chicken or cheese, coated in breadcrumbs and deep fried. It'll be the size and shape of a large pear. On its own, it will keep a diet-conscious person going all morning and possibly well into the afternoon too. A Brazilian, however, will often devour at least a couple just as a snack – and they are really very good. As I said, you need to find a good *padaria* – but every city and neighbourhood in Brazil seems to have one that locals claim make the best *cozinhas* in the world.

The other fried food you'll find for breakfast is *pastel* – plural *pasteis* – a rectangular pastry package stuffed with cheese, ham, or more or less anything edible, and fried until crisp. They come in miniature as a snack, and in a bar they might serve you a portion of a dozen of them, but visit the *padaria* and you'll find 'regular' ones that are about 10 x 15 cm in their dimensions.

With so much fried food on offer, you may well ask why the shops that make them are called bakeries – but bread is a highly important part of the Brazilian breakfast too. *Pao de queijo* – cheese bread – is a speciality unique to Brazil. They are little balls, about 3cm in diameter, made of cassava flour and cheese, and eaten puffed, crisp and warm from the oven – they're very moreish.

Naturally there is regular bread too, usually white and very airy and light, and almost always – at least for hotel breakfasts – turned into cheese and ham sandwiches.

And to finish breakfast – though for quite a lot of Brazilians it's also to begin – there's cake. Lots of cake. The more basic hotels may not have much or any choice of *petiscos*, and the *pao de queijo* may have been grabbed by earlier breakfasters, but I can guarantee they'll have plenty of cake.

To go with the cake, there's always coffee. 'There's an awful lot of coffee in Brazil' and they sure do drink a lot of it, all through the day, in small espresso-sized quantities – the *cafezinho*. Brazilian coffee is famous – outside Brazil. In the country itself, they're pretty good at destroying most of its aroma and any of its subtlety. While, even for home use, one can buy filter and espresso machines, Brazilian hotels, cafes and offices usually make coffee in big boilers, creating an extremely black, thick and strong brew that almost invariably comes ready-sweetened. I love coffee – even stewed-to-death Brazilian coffee – but I don't take sugar, so the very first words of Portuguese that I had to learn to pronounce correctly were "*sem açucar*" (without sugar). Although getting that is rarely a problem in hotels, in many offices – and all the car factories I visited on this trip – the only choice was either stand-your-spoon-up-in-it sweetened, or nothing.

After that calorie-intensive breakfast, I expect you're wondering how Brazilians survive until lunchtime. But, somehow, they do. And at that feeding opportunity there's another carbohydrate hit, in the form of rice and beans – *feijões*. It is, in fact, a staple across the whole of Latin America, although the type of beans used varies a bit, presumably depending on availability and season, but they are always small, dark red or black, and the principles of cooking and eating are the same. A large scoop of white rice doused with another of beans is a fundamental component of people's lunch most days. It's almost always the first thing put on the plate in factory and office canteens – the provision of lunch for staff is a legal requirement of employers in Brazil

That doesn't mean that there aren't plenty of places to eat out, and they get pretty busy. If all you want is a sandwich, there are takeaway *lanchonetes* everywhere. The name doesn't actually have anything to do with lunch – a *lanche* is a sandwich, or, rather, a large bap.

Although they exist in some other countries, *por quilo* (per-kilo) restaurants are ubiquitous in Brazil, and, unless you've got a staff canteen or are content with a *lanche*, they're the go-to choice at lunchtime. They're self-service buffets – you pick up a plate and help yourself to whatever you want from what's on offer, then take it to the cashier who weighs it and charges you 'per kilo' for the food you've taken. There's just one price so, gram for gram, you're paying the same for rice and beans as you are for meat or fish or salad. There's always a big sign up showing the price per kilo and the standard weight of an empty plate (pick one that's chipped to get a few extra grams of food free and ignore hygiene concerns!). There's a big variation in quality and choice between restaurants but, just like everywhere else in the world, the busiest ones are inevitably the best.

Ones with better choice are also usually more expensive, though still amazing value.

Even when going to an upmarket eatery there's no need to worry that you won't get your rice and beans! Other staples you'll always find and either love or loathe are *manioca* (in English-speaking countries, usually called cassava root or yam) – great when deep fried, rather stodgy when just boiled – and cabbage, finely shredded and boiled to death. The good news is that there'll be salad, meat, fish and, if you're lucky, interesting things like sushi too.

On some weekdays, you might even find what many Brazilians regard as the ultimate weekend lunch – *feijoada*. It's a heavy bean stew with added meat and sausage (especially sausage), eaten with rice and cabbage. *Manioca* too – but this time in a distinct form, dried and shredded, and called *farofa*. The reason it's considered a weekend lunch is that the only thing you'll want to do after eating a plateful is to take a siesta. Be warned, therefore, not to over-indulge if you find it on the lunchtime buffet and you need to work in the afternoon.

Dinner time – or maybe Sunday lunch – is when the finest in Brazilian dining comes out. As you'd expect, different restaurants serve different cuisines. However, one common theme stands out – and that's the *rodizio*. The literal translation is 'rotation', and that's exactly what happens. Waiters keep coming around with different things, you take what you fancy and then, a bit later, accept a different morsel from another one. And so it goes on until you stop them. There's a device on each table – usually a red and green disc – which you set to green when you're hungry and red when you're not, to keep the waiters away.

Brazilian-style restaurants in the UK and USA have the same, but whereas in my experience you might have to wait five or ten minutes for a solitary waiter to come past, in Brazil turning the disc to green indicates that it's feeding time at the zoo, and a whole horde of waiters with different delicacies are likely to descend all at once. This is good, because you can be picky and choose the bits you fancy most; I'm sure the reason that the British equivalents only have a single waiter at infrequent intervals is to get diners to eat cheaper cuts, or offload leftovers, or both.

Rodizios are also for the hungry – you can eat as much as you want for a fixed price, and many do gorge themselves. Many restaurants, recognising that one partner is likely to eat much less than the other, have a 'couples' price. And kids go free, or for a bargain price – until it comes to desserts, which aren't included in the price, and inevitably carry a premium price tag.

For the carnivore, there is nothing quite like a Brazilian *churrasco,* the original and classic *rodizio*. It's their one cuisine that attracts world fame. South Americans in general love their meat, Brazilians more than most amongst their neighbours, though perhaps not quite as much as Argentinians and Uruguayans, for whom beef is a religion.

There's nothing unique about grilling meat – it's the technique and presentation that makes it different. The most iconic cut that one sees in pictures is *picanha* – beef sirloin, cut into 15cm thick joints, three or four of them skewered on a sword and barbecued in a pit. As the outside layer of meat crisps, the sword is borne in left hand by a brave waiter, clutching a dagger (OK, carving knife) in his right, and brought to tables where the meat is sliced off thinly. The crispy outside has a delicious barbecued flavour. The downside is that it also gives you a massive salt hit, perhaps inadvisable for those with high blood pressure. Diners who prefer roast beef in varying stages of rareness go for later slices. After the first few slices have been served from the sword, the waiter returns it to the pit for the meat to be barbecued again.

But, it's not just *picanha* that you get. Oh, no! There are many different cuts of beef alone, and in a posher restaurant they'll serve most of them. As a foreigner, they'll likely give you a card with a 'cow map' showing which bit comes from where and what they're called. There's also chicken, lamb, ham and, the *pièce de résistance* for many Brazilians, chicken hearts, threaded onto thin rapier swords in their hundreds.

For variety – and for any suffering vegetarians who may inadvertently be present – there is always a big buffet counter heaving with salads, and perhaps other dishes; but meat is king.

For dessert? Pineapple dusted with cinnamon and grilled on a sword.

Not a carnivore? Try pizza. I'm a huge fan of Brazilian pizza. Surely pizzas are the same the world over? Unquestionably not. As you'd expect, there are all sorts of toppings available – and the whole point of a *rodizio* service is to try them all (well, several) – but the big difference in Brazil is cheese. Still mozzarella cheese, but masses of it. You know the adverts for pizza restaurants at home, with the picture of a slice of pizza dangling long, stretchy, sinewy strands of cheese? Then you go to the same restaurant chain and find it's impossible to recreate? That's never a problem in Brazil. In fact, there is no skimping on any of the toppings.

Pizzas are big, fully loaded and very cheesy – and if you go on *rodizio* night, and your appetite is up to it, you can try lots. Not a *rodizio* night, but in the mood for variety? No problem, you can get a bespoke pizza all to yourselves and have it subdivided into three or four different toppings of your choice. Huge and delicious.

Brazilians are such pizzaholics that they've even invented dessert pizzas. Instead of tomato sauce and cheese, think chocolate and fruit (perhaps there is a place in this world for pineapple on pizza!).

Beyond meat and pizza, there are plenty of other options. Everyone knows Brazil is famous as the 'Rainbow Nation', and each wave of immigrants in the 19th and early 20th century brought its own cuisine with it. Each was adapted to local ingredients and evolved over the following century, so some are now only vaguely recognisable.

The Italians brought pizza to Brazil, but they also introduced *parmigiana*. It's very popular in Brazil, though the dish is no longer much like its European ancestor. Take thin beef steaks, beat them flat, egg and breadcrumb them, fry them – so far, it's schnitzel – put them as a base layer in a deep baking tray, spread tomato sauce thickly over that, then cover with a mountain of cheese, maybe sprinkle breadcrumbs on top, and bake until sizzling. Meat and breadless pizza all in the same dish!

The Portuguese brought *bacalhau* – salt cod. Prepared in a myriad of ways, these dishes remain the closest to the originals, probably because of the overwhelming Portuguese influence; after all, Brazil was once a colony. But I find it surprising that there aren't more restaurants dedicated to *bacalhau*.

Another favourite is Japanese. There are lots of Japanese restaurants in São Paulo state, because there are a lot of Japanese people living there. A million of them arrived in the early 1900s when there was a famine; they came as agricultural workers and started the coffee plantations. Although there's been intermarriage in the past century, many stayed culturally tied, and today there are at least three million who have pure Japanese blood. These divide into 'true' Japanese (the ones who can speak and write the language) and 'fake' Japanese (the majority who only speak and write Portuguese). But whether true or fake, they run and patronise lots of Japanese restaurants.

Back home, Japanese restaurants are expensive. In Brazil, whilst they're more costly compared to other cuisines, they're still very affordable – and, best of all, most are *rodizio*, so you can eat as much sushi, sashimi, yakitori and tempura as you like for a set price.

Naturally, you'll want to wash this all down with a nice drink – and in Brazil the favourite is beer. Beer served very, very cold. '*Estupidamente gelada*', as locals say. When it's draught, it's served in small glasses – about 200ml – and called *chopp*. To prove it's going to be cold, the beer taps have digital thermometers on the front of them, typically showing around -3°C. Much more common is for couples or groups to share large bottles (650ml), pouring into very small glasses. It's a tropical country, so beer needs to stay cold – the bottles are often served in ice buckets, and more commonly still with an insulating foam polystyrene sleeve, colloquially called a *camisinha* (condom). Expensive bars and restaurants serve half-size bottles (at full size prices), like the ones we find in Europe and North America, called long-necks.

There are lots of brands of beer, but Skol and Brahma dominate the market. Personally, I've avoided Brahma since I was introduced to it on my first business visit to Brazil and blamed it for a terrible headache that I woke up with on the following day. It wasn't that I'd drunk too much of it, of course!

I do have my definite favourite, though – *Original*. Whilst I've somewhat gone off beer when I'm at home or anywhere else in the world, I can and do drink a lot of *bem gelada* (well chilled) Original when I am in Brazil. Just writing about it now makes me miss it. That and *picanha*... what I'd give for a *churrasco* dinner right now!

However much I love things Brazilian, their wine proves that there are some things that a country just can't and shouldn't even try to do. I suppose the sparkling wine is OK if you like semi-sweet weak prosecco and you're in a party where the quality is immaterial, but I warn readers to avoid local red and white wines. Better restaurants serve good stuff from Argentina and Chile, but for some reason, despite Mercosur, they're expensive.

The national spirit is *cachaça*, distilled from sugar cane (so related to rum). The cheapest stuff (the best-known brand being '51') is clear white alcohol with all the attraction of paintbrush cleaner, but even that becomes perfectly acceptable when poured over a glassful of crushed limes and sugar to make the national cocktail, caipirinha.

There's very good cachaça to be found, and some bars have shelves and shelves with perhaps a thousand different varieties. Most of the good stuff comes from the region of Minas Gerais (the mines themselves are of iron ore, but the region is better known in Brazil for its cheese and cachaça).

Usually a golden colour, it's a pleasure to drink neat or, in a popular and lethal combination, as a chaser to chilled beer.

The temptation has got to me, writing this. Excuse me while I go to the drinks cupboard and pour myself a shot for old times' sake! *Saude*! And then… back to my story of business.

WEEK 1 - DAY 3
A WILD GOOSE CHASE,
AND A DRIVE THROUGH A STORM

Another day, another car factory. This one was an easy and quick drive from my hotel. I'd stopped at a petrol station and bought a real map (something else I should have done on the first day) and, in my opinion at least, was fast becoming an expert in Brazilian roads and traffic. It was a lazy start too; my contact, Franco, had said he couldn't meet me before 11am. I no longer had faith in Mapquest, which estimated 45 minutes for the journey, but even doubling that I still didn't need to leave the hotel until 9.30am.

Twenty minutes later, I started to have misgivings, as the route seemed to lead me away from civilisation on a fairly narrow road through interminable, dense forest. At least it wasn't a busy highway. I stopped and checked the map again, crossed my fingers, kept going, and finally, another twenty minutes later, reached a clearing – and the factory. Nothing else in sight, apart from forest. So, today,

Mapquest had proved more or less right, as I'd arrived more than half an hour early.

I'd assumed this would be a big factory like the others, but it looked to be not much more than a very large shed amidst acres of asphalt, over which were scattered hundreds of huge metal blocks of all shapes and sizes. Viewed from afar, it resembled some sort of sculpture park. A very industrial one.

Being so early, I had plenty of time, perched on an uncomfortable stool in the guard hut at the gate, to twiddle my thumbs and wonder what the blocks of metal were for. At least this time I could be sure I was at the right gate; the guard told me it was the only one. What a contrast to the day before; this one was not only friendly, he wanted to chat. He jabbered non-stop for several minutes. I'd have been happy to join in, but my minimal Portuguese made small talk impossible. Once he'd realised that I hadn't understood a word he'd said, we reverted to stony silence, him standing behind his desk staring into the distance, willing someone, anyone, to come out of the forest and give him somebody to talk to; me sat in the corner, fidgeting to try to get comfortable, wondering how much longer I'd have to wait. Outside, nothing seemed to move. All was still. So much so, I began to wonder if the plant had closed down and I was wasting my time.

But, a few minutes after eleven, Franco arrived. Once we'd greeted each other and he'd led me past the gate, it became clear that the 'factory' was just a huge, largely empty, shed. Franco explained it doubled as a warehouse and a press shop. That's where huge mechanical stamping machines are used to turn flat sheets of steel into car body parts. What I'd seen as a sculpture park was in fact a sort of industrial cemetery, the last resting place for the moulded dies once used in the stamping presses to make the bodies of cars that were now obsolete.

When any of those cars that were still on the road had crashes (and, from my experience, that must have been a regular occurrence), repair shops ordered replacement body shell mouldings from here. The relevant dies would be located somewhere on the lot, loaded into one of those big presses, and they'd stamp out the panels that were needed. Now the workers had returned from their break, forklift trucks were moving around the asphalt, picking up a die here and dropping another there, like some sort of monster chess game.

All very fascinating, insofar as it was different from any of the other factories I'd visited. But the fascination only lasted around five minutes. I'd toured the entire plant, learned all I would ever need to know about stamping out replacement car body parts, and it still wasn't 11.30. Not even time for lunch. But then, naturally, I still had to get the bills. Franco and I set off to meet the admin manager, Thais, to ask for them.

Thais was very charming, greeting each of us with a hug, but brightly told us that she didn't have them. Yes, the bills came to her, but then she sent them on to the bigger plant – the one I had been at yesterday. And no, she didn't keep copies. Her friend at the big plant had told her I'd been there yesterday, and had asked why I hadn't picked them up while I was there? Well, because I didn't know, nobody asked, and nobody said…

Happily, there was a straightforward solution. One of her colleagues was about to drive over from the other plant and could bring them with him. She assured me that by the time I'd had lunch he'd definitely be there, as he had a 2pm meeting.

It would have been easy to stretch out lunch for hours had I known anything about Brazilian football – or any kind of football, come to that. Most people I've met in São Paulo state, men and women equally, support either São Paulo FC or Corinthians. Other teams exist, but their supporters must live in places I haven't visited. Franco was a Corinthian fan. Big time. Earlier, he'd shown me the photo of him with the team proudly hanging on the wall over his desk, where all possible bric-à-brac – mug, mouse mat, pen holder and so on – sported (sic) their logo, which looks something like an anchor with crossed oars. Afterwards, as we met anyone as we walked around, Franco would conspiratorially whisper to tell me if they were SPFC supporters, AKA 'The Enemy'.

Sadly, in the course of our lunchtime conversation, I believe I got grouped with that huge band of misguided individuals. I don't support any team. I don't even like football. But that was obviously the wrong thing to tell him. In Franco's world, soccer agnosticism equated to being a covert SPFC supporter. And I couldn't shift the conversation on to any other topic. Football, and specifically Corinthianism, was his life.

Finally, nourished with rice and beans, armed with copies of bills, and having exhausted nearly a whole minute examining the electricity meter in detail, and perhaps five minutes more walking around the perimeter of the building to look at all the light switches, I'd achieved what I'd come to do. Many business trips involve considerable travel and time consumed for what in the end feels like very little result but, nevertheless, it had been worthwhile. Neither I nor my colleagues would have understood this operation if I hadn't gone and seen it for myself.

Well before 3pm, I was back on the road, facing a long drive to another new destination at a difficult time of day. On Brazilian roads with Brazilian drivers.

When I'd originally planned the itinerary, before I'd left London, I'd thought that the place where I was today was west of São Paulo, and that my next destination was further west still – so this morning's visit would be 'on the way'. I'd screwed up (again). I suppose I'd had the map upside down, or I'd confused the place name – when it comes to Brazilian towns named after saints, there's an awful lot of repetition.

In fact, my visit of the morning had been in the opposite direction, east. If I'd planned better, it would have made more sense to have moved hotel the day before and stay nearby to this factory. But I hadn't. So now I had to retrace my steps. Drive towards São Paulo, drive past it, and then go a further 100km west to my next city, and find the hotel where I was going to stay that night, ready for the next day's site visit. All in the early evening rush hour.

Mapquest's estimation of a 90-minute total journey time was hopelessly optimistic, and perhaps only achievable by Ayrton Senna himself, in the early hours of the morning with no traffic and breaking all the speed limits. And definitely not possible in my rental car, which, on the few occasions it found itself on an uncongested open road, complained at any speed above 60 km/hr. Anyway, I wasn't in a hurry; I just wanted to arrive before the restaurant closed and in time to get my notes in order before bed. Best to take it easy.

So, double the estimated time. Three hours. I'd be there by 6pm or so, I thought, piles of time.

Ha. The first 30 or 40km, back through the forest, was quick enough – but then I reached the perpetual impasse of the São Paulo 'ring road'. In one sense, it's not dissimilar to the South and North Circular London ring road. An uninformed visitor, looking at a map, might see it as one road. It's not.

In the case of São Paulo, there are at least three conjoined roads that create the 'ring'. The northern part, running straight east to west, joins the westerly part, running straight south to north. Both follow the banks of rivers, so are called 'marginals'. The eastern and southern parts are bits of other roads, presumably joined to the others as they go in the right direction. The whole ring is basically just horrible, and nothing like a ring.

For my drive west to Sorocaba, I only needed to cover the northern part – all the way from east to west. Just 20km.

That 'north of the river' section in São Paulo closely follows the river Tiete, with the westbound carriageway on one side and the eastbound on the other. The Tiete is indeed a river – but it looks more like a wide drainage canal. Apart from the flotsam and jetsam floating on the river and the garbage lining the banks, there's usually dirty foam on the surface, giving the impression – perhaps true, I never checked – that the effluent from a detergent factory is dumped directly into the river. Every few years, there's a clean-up plan. Passers-by are only aware because of the 'new clean up plan' signs that are put up. The river then looks better for a short while before the signs rust or fall down, and the river reverts to type.

If the traffic moved at any normal speed, one wouldn't have time to look and see the state of the Tiete. But it doesn't, or it didn't back then – I admit that there have been some changes that have been quite effective in speeding up traffic in the last few years. At the time, driving west to east or east to west, drivers had at least an hour, often two or three, to enjoy the view as they stopped and started along the whole tedious 20 kilometres.

The slow speed had nothing to do with the width of the road. It was mostly what road traffic reporters on British radio call 'sheer weight of traffic'. Add the inevitable broken-down truck – or, worse, one that has spilt its load all over the carriageway – and one has a recipe for a slow crawl. In the rush hour, add a motorcycle accident – very common – and paralysis ensues.

On this occasion, all those ingredients of an interminable journey were present. Plus one more.

The dark cloud I'd seen looming ahead as I drove towards SP wasn't just pollution caused by stationary traffic. It was a veritable cloud. A very black cloud. Prompt on 5 o'clock, lightning lit up the sky, thunder rolled and sudden torrential rain descended. Teeming. Inundatory. Scaturient. There are no words accurate enough to describe a tropical storm to those who haven't experienced one. At certain times of year, they're very common in Brazil – to the extent that, even if it's not quite safe to set one's clock by them, one can rely on one starting at around about 5pm most afternoons.

In a car, it's bad enough if you're stationary. If you're moving, as I was, you have to stop. There's no choice. Visibility drops to zero in an instant. It's so dangerous. In just a few seconds, bright daylight transitions to obscure darkness. That means cars don't have their lights on. Latin American drivers are firmly of the belief that car lights run down the battery, and won't turn them on at any time unless essential. Also, back then, many cars and trucks had broken lights, or such weak ones that they were of little use at any time. In a tropical downpour, the sky, the rain, the road, all those cars uniformly painted silver, everything looks the same. Slate grey. Wipers are useless. It is impossible to describe the horror of driving, even at a meagre 20km per hour, in the middle lane of a six-lane road, closely surrounded by other vehicles on all sides, and suddenly losing all visibility. Brake and stop? Be hit by the one behind you. Keep going? Hit the one in front. Hobson had better choices.

I didn't collide with anything, thanks to luck or providence or intervention of some invisible Star Fleet deflector shield, but that part of the journey, the first storm I'd experienced while driving in Brazil, lives on in my memory. How I got to the hotel itself, having reached the city of Sorocaba, doesn't. I never expected to return ever again, but a few years later, through one of those quirks of fate, I ended up living there for many months every year over a ten-year period. Thinking back now about that city, spread out over a vast area with countless rambling roads, I think that it must have been some kind of personal miracle that I ever found the hotel that night.

Sorocaba is not the sort of place holidaymakers would visit, but there is a tourist office in the library, presumably to provide maps to those who are lost (though, if so, it's unlikely they'd ever find the library).

The journey had taken five hours. Later I was told that the traffic must have been light because it would usually take six or seven!

Fortunately, me being hungry and thirsty, the hotel restaurant and bar was still open when I arrived. There was no menu; the only food on offer was a burger. No problem there though; I'd have eaten anything. The place was packed, but I think I was the only person eating. I figured out that they were all travelling salesmen – it didn't take much power of observation, as they are, or were, the same the world over. A lot of beer was being drunk, and it was very noisy. I became quite the object of attention – despite the size of the city, a foreigner who didn't speak Portuguese was something of a rarity.

Either that, or the other foreigners had found better places to stay. The hotel was modern, it even belonged to a chain, but the room was a cell. Plain white walls, a hard bed, and a shelf masquerading as a miniscule worktop. No chair; to use the worktop as a desk meant perching on the end of the bed.

I'd chosen the hotel because it was the only one in the city that I could find online that claimed to have internet in the rooms. Not Wi-Fi, mind. In return for a cash deposit, the receptionist gave me a sort of modem I'd never seen before, a black brick with cables hanging out of it. It looked ancient even then. She demonstrated, largely by sign language, that I should disconnect the TV antenna cable and plug it in to that. That was straightforward enough, although, since the TV was screwed high up the wall, I now had the device dangling down from it carrying its own weight. It had two more cables. The RJ45 connection to the computer was straightforward too – but only just reached the worktop. The third cable was for power.

Since I already had the laptop plugged in, I'd need the only remaining socket in the room, which was the one for the TV. Not only was it awkwardly right behind it, but near the top of the wall. It proved to be quite a performance standing on the bed to remove one plug and insert the other.

Performance is the word, as the moment I plugged it in, the modem exploded. Well, let's be realistic. There was a small bang, and smoke came out of it.

This was when I discovered that although most power sockets in Brazil are 127 volts, some of them are 220 volts, and the same plugs fit both. Nobody had told me. Apparently, I'd picked the wrong one.

I then found out that my computer had died too. Shouldn't have happened, no technical explanation, but it did. That meant I was now going to be without a laptop for the rest of my trip round South America. I had a Blackberry, but that only worked in the countries that had compatible mobile phone signals, Brazil not being one of them. As I've said, there was no Wi-Fi in 2002…

WEEK 1 - DAY 4
BRAZIL; THE MORNING AFTER THE NIGHT BEFORE

I spent the first couple of hours of the morning discovering what a big city Sorocaba was, from getting lost and driving for miles in various wrong directions, to looking for a factory that, when I found it, turned out to be just a warehouse. Apart from what I went for, it gave me my first opportunity to meet some of the Japanese population of Brazil.

My contacts at the site were two brothers. In their mid-30's, I guessed, and quite corpulent, they created in my mind the image of a middle-aged, Japanese version of Tweedledum and Tweedledee that lived with me for years afterwards, even though I never saw them again beyond that day. Their real names were Yoshi and Ishi; just as well it was a brief visit and I didn't need to talk to them a lot, as I had no hope of remembering who was who.

Not much energy gets used in a warehouse in a tropical country. It was just a large, high shed, filled to the roof with parts for cars. The only electricity they needed was for lights and mechanical handling equipment (forklift trucks). A little air conditioning for the offices. One bill a month. Always more or less the same usage and cost, month after month. Once I was in their office, it took less than a minute to find a nice person who promised to scan and email to us a copy of that rather uninteresting bill every month thereafter.

Having completed my mission for the day in thirty minutes, I faced a five-or-six-hour drive back the way I'd come, to São Paulo's Guarulhos airport. It would have been nice to have flown out of Sorocaba – it does have an airport – and, had I been there just one week earlier, it would have been possible. Before I left London, I'd discovered a flight and even managed to reserve a seat. But, by the time I woke up the next morning, the airline had gone bust. Or maybe sunk – I think it was called Ocean Air.

That was no surprise. Airlines in Brazil (and, for that matter, the rest of South America) were well known for having very short lifespans. As recently as two years ago, taxiing in to São Paulo's Guarulhos airport, one could see, parked on the edges of the airfield, the deteriorating hulks of ancient planes painted in the liveries of airlines that had disappeared from the skies twenty years earlier.

Anyway, there was no flight, and I don't think there have been any scheduled passenger flights on any airline leaving Sorocaba since then. Having seen everything there was to see at the warehouse, and still feeling full of cake from breakfast, I turned down the invitation to a beans-and-rice canteen lunch and got back on the road. I needed to get moving anyway – I had a flight at 7pm which I'd reserved not knowing, until the previous day's traumatic drive, that it was going to take so long to reach the airport. In the end, I missed it anyway.

A few weeks later, though, I was entertainingly reminded of returning the car on that evening to the rental company at Guarulhos. Or rather, the act of refuelling it before I did so. Not something one would expect to be amused by.

Having returned to my London office, an amiable lady in our finance department offered to do my expenses. Very kind of her – I was good at collecting receipts, little bits of paper, but not so good at getting around to transcribing them onto expense forms, mainly because I found looking up cost centre codes for everything so tedious. When she came to tell me she'd finished, she shyly remarked that I seemed to have spent an unusually large amount on entertainment in Brazil, but none in any other country on my trip. Had my meetings involved getting lots of people drunk? This was surprising. I didn't remember entertaining anybody – and certainly not getting anyone (even myself) drunk.

My first thought was that I must have picked up someone else's receipts – but then she showed me the offending ones. Little slips showing that what I'd bought was 'Alcool'. Yes, alcohol. Just alcohol. But not the marvellous stuff you drink, the poisonous kind that cars run on.

At Brazilian filling stations, you have a choice between gasoline and alcohol (now renamed 'ethanol') when you refuel your car. Way back in the 1970s, Brazil pioneered the use of alcohol as a motor fuel, when a global fuel crisis raised petrol prices and created shortages. The first alcohol-fuelled cars went into production around 1976 and, for many years now, all cars sold there are 'Flex', meaning they can run on alcohol, gasoline or any mixture of the two. Some say that it reduces performance and fuel economy, but most Brazilians buy alcohol because it's much cheaper.

In Brazil, ethanol/alcohol was produced locally from sugar cane. Now, in other countries, it's made from rapeseed, corn, soya and other crops as well. I'm not sure that it's as ecologically responsible as it sounds, as one needs masses of sugar cane or soya beans to make enough alcohol to fill a tank, so they have turned millions of hectares of land over to growing it. The insatiable demand for agricultural land, no longer just to feed people, is a primary factor driving the destruction of the Amazon.

My accounts colleague, who was asking about my business boozing, naturally didn't know that it was a substitute for petrol. On more recent visits to Brazil, I've always wondered if the reason they renamed alcohol to ethanol was to avoid drivers on company expenses becoming embarrassed when cross-examined about their drinking habits by eagle-eyed accountants.

WEEK 1 - DAY 5
SEEKING NIRVANA IN THE AIRPORT

Since I'd missed my evening flight, I'd stayed the night at the same hotel near Guarulhos airport that I'd struggled to reach on my first night in Brazil. I'd returned my rental car first, rebooked my flight for the next morning and taken the shuttle bus to the hotel. Now I could see where I'd missed the turning. A simple route when you know how.

The plane wasn't due to leave until 11am, so I had plenty of time to explore and enjoy the airport before boarding and take off. I could have gone to a lounge, but I had no desire to escape the crowds; in fact, quite the opposite. I checked in, went through security, worked out my route to the gate for later, then picked the busier of the two cafes in the main concourse, sat at a table right at the front, ordered a coffee and a plate of *pao de queijo*, and sat back to enjoy the sights.

I love airports. Others think I'm crazy, perhaps you do too, but I really do. Small ones, huge ones, single terminals, multi-terminals… cities in themselves, with thousands of workers going about their business, at all hours of day and night, some dedicated to making our journeys possible, others to robbing us of our money in overpriced shops and cafes before we fly or after we land. I'm fascinated by how an airport runs seamlessly as one huge well-oiled machine, and to watch how, when things go wrong, as they do all the time, all those little crises are fixed by people running around like the T-cells of a mammalian immune system dealing with infections before they have a chance to get out of control.

Sure, I dislike hassles, queues and hanging around aimlessly as much as anyone else – but in airports I actually enjoy the waits; it's an ideal time and place for people-watching. The best place of all for the biggest variety of people.

People of all nationalities – I try to guess which, looking to see what clues they reveal, perhaps sneaking a surreptitious glance at their passport cover to prove whether I got it right. People of different ages, some calm and relaxed, lots of them stressed and tetchy.

Looking at what people wear to travel; their fashion sense, or lack of it; are they trying to make a statement, or just dressing for comfort? Going from one climate to another, are they dressed for departure or arrival?

Trying to be an amateur psychologist and determining what a person's hand luggage says about them.

People with luminescent orange-and-pink wheely cases that you see in the shops and know someone somewhere has to be buying, but until now couldn't imagine who.

Optimistic and opportunist people with bulging backpacks that obviously exceed the hand-baggage size limits but are determined to try to take them on board with them.

People stuffing bags inside other bags and donning sweaters, jackets and coats even on a stifling summer's day, because the budget airline only lets them take one piece of hand baggage.

People nervously and repeatedly picking up and putting down their bag, worrying that it'll get weighed at the gate and be over the permitted allowance.

Gate agents in a jobsworth mood at 5 o'clock in the morning who take the opportunity to wind up passengers by checking absolutely everything, and the same ones at the end of the day, desperate to get off, simply past caring and waving everyone through.

People checking in with vast quantities of luggage, hoping that they'll not have to pay excess.

People trying to retrieve massive cases from crowded carousels that are moving just that bit too fast for them.

The show-off businessman (it's always a man) hovering at the front of the boarding line with an economy ticket and Group 7 boarding pass, talking loudly enough into his phone to give away all his trade secrets just in the hope that the gate agent will not want to interrupt and will let him through with Group 1.

Happy young couples too busy snogging to notice that the plane is on last call and having to be nudged apart by a gate agent.

Hassled mothers trying to cope with playful youngsters running out of control and away from the gate while their fathers concentrate on a magazine or their phone and pretend that they're not together.

People of all ages who've fallen asleep, despite the discomfort of airport benches, having given up on all hope of their perpetually delayed flight ever boarding.

A few souls defiantly refusing a buggy ride, but almost defeated by the struggle of the endeavour of making it as far as Gate 99.

Immigration officers whose minds are obviously elsewhere, hardly glancing at passports and seemingly just there to stamp them.

Other immigration officers determined to give every passenger a hard time, checking every page in the passport, asking both relevant and irrelevant questions, denying entry to the victim's promised land until the very last minute.

All human life is there! So many people, so many scenes, so much opportunity to enjoy the company of our fellow members of the global human race and see the differences – and the many more similarities – between us.

And in a foreign airport, watching people is even more fascinating. I nearly missed my flight to Caracas!

WEEK 2 - DAY 0
ARRIVING IN VENEZUELA AND AVOIDING KIDNAP

My local hosts in Venezuela had been most insistent that I couldn't drive myself. The hundred-kilometre road between Caracas airport and Valencia, my destination, looked to be a straightforward drive on the only map I could find when browsing in Stanfords back in London. But since it was going to be my first visit to the country, and the route was beyond the exploration limits of Mapquest, I'd been happy to accept their offer. I'd assumed they were just being polite. But no; once in the car and on our way, the driver told me the real reason was that they were scared someone might kidnap me.

It hadn't occurred to me that might be a risk. The very little recent news I'd read of the Bolivarian Republic (as it was then called) suggested that it was undergoing something of an economic revolution. There's no doubt that the country ought to be rich – it does, after all, sit on the world's largest known oil reserves – and old societal inequalities were fast being reduced. At least, that's what it said on the government website.

However, my customer, a big American corporation, wasn't quite as optimistic as President Hugo Chavez. They weren't going to take the risk that some lowlife for whom the revolution had not yet delivered riches might spot a very white, very non-Venezuelan visitor arriving at the airport and suppose that he looked like a good bet for a big ransom demand. Hence, I was met at the airport, literally right at the exit door coming from customs, by a burly, uniformed – and visibly armed – driver. He looked very scary. At first, I thought he was a policeman. I hadn't expected to be kidnapped, but I hadn't expected to be arrested either! Least of all met by someone with an AK47 slung round their shoulder.

Fortunately, despite first appearances, my driver was very polite and charming, and extremely relieved to find out that I spoke Spanish, as his few words of English stretched little beyond 'good evening'. He introduced himself as Miguel.

As a bodyguard, Miguel looked professional, but the car he was driving was anything but. It was a huge American thing with wings, at least 10 years old, perhaps 20, but polished to a gleam. It might have been old, but once we were away from the airport and on the main road, it was obvious that, by local standards, this was a relatively upmarket vehicle. There were newer cars around, sure, but most were ancient, not so much pre-loved as pre-bashed, belching out fumes. As a carscape, it was reminiscent of Cuba a decade earlier, except that while the cars were almost certainly rather newer, they were definitely worse maintained. The smoke these ones spewed out made Brazilian trucks seem environmentally friendly.

Miguel explained that most people bought second-hand cars shipped in from the States. Since petrol was only around eight cents per gallon, who cared about the fuel consumption? And why maintain cars so they used less? As long as they kept moving and were cheap...

The plight of the poor may have been improving through the Boliviaran Revolution, but these old bangers, coupled with the sight of the Caracas suburbs as we drove through them, made it clear to me that its aims hadn't yet been fully realised. The gulf between rich and poor was as blatant as in other semi-developed countries I'd visited – Kenya seemed a good comparison. No: Mexico – very much a Latin American country!

I was impressed that the hotel my plant contact had booked for me seemed so posh. The fact that Valencia actually had a five-star hotel, and that it belonged to a major chain, InterContinental, had led me to expect that the city would be prosperous and I'd be rubbing shoulders with the rich and famous, even if the room rate did seem unbelievably cheap.

I may not have been the only guest, but there weren't many others – I only saw maybe three or four, all members of the travelling salesman fraternity. The hotel certainly had grandeur, and was set in beautiful tropical gardens that were a pleasure to wander around in early evening. There were lots of birds, and a few little furry animals scurrying for cover. One of the many times I wished I'd had a camera with me.

With armed guards on the hotel gates, and having had a lecture from Miguel on the risks of kidnapping, it obviously wasn't a safe idea to wander out exploring and looking for dinner; this evening's feast was going to be whatever I fancied off the hotel menu. Which wasn't very inspiring; they'd obviously pruned it down since their better days to things that they could rustle up quickly from the freezer for the few guests they now had. All 'international fare', as hospitality likes to call it; roughly translated as burgers, chicken nuggets and pizza.

Pepe, the waiter, looked well past retirement age, and had probably spent all his working life waiting on tables here since the hotel was first built. As I was the only diner, he was more than willing to chat. I told him it was my first visit to Venezuela, and knew nothing about the cuisine – but surely local people ate different things to burgers and pizzas? Morosely, he told me about better times past, the fine meals that families would prepare, and the big parties the hotel used to host. I was resigning myself to a burger, but then he brightened and asked if I had tried *arepas*. No, I had no concept of what an *arepa* was. And thus I was introduced to what I understand to be Venezuela's greatest contribution to international cuisine.

Pepe scuttled off to the kitchen and returned to tell me that the chef would prepare me a special *arepa*, the *Reina Pepiada*. I was game for anything. Just the name sounded interesting.

Inquiring of Pepe, I learnt that '*Pepiada*' is a Venezuelan term for anything that's wonderful or special, or, in the case of women, curvaceous. The *reina*, or queen, in this context is allegedly a Venezuelan Miss Universe of the 1950s in whose honour this *arepa* was created.

Just talking about this was making Pepe nostalgic. "We always had the Miss Valencia pageant here," he said wistfully. "Such beautiful young women. We had many waiters then. We all used to fight amongst ourselves to get to serve the top tables."

Pepe was obviously an old school character and a bit of a lecher. "Surely today's young women are just as beautiful?" I replied.

"Of course, but there are no beauty parades any more, no glamourous events. They're not allowed. Señor Chavez keeps all the girls for himself." Pepe rambled on; he was plainly of the belief that Government House had been converted into a brothel for the country's leaders. "And we see no young women here in the hotel at all any more. I am very sorry."

It made sense that there might be no more beauty parades, even in macho South American countries, but no women working or staying in the hotel? Ever?

"You must have some working here in the hotel. I'm sure Venezuela is full of clever young women," I said. I was pretty sure the receptionist when I arrived had been female.

"Of course, some of them are very good, very beautiful, very clever. I have a card somewhere. I can give you the number to call."

Innocent me; I was very slow on the uptake. "No, it's OK, I am just here to work," I replied.

He shrugged and went off to the kitchen to fetch my *arepa*. It turned out to be a stuffed pancake. Well, a sort of pancake. An *arepa* pancake is made of yellow maize flour; it's quite thick, around 6mm I'd say, puffy, fried to golden on both sides and folded over a stuffing. That could be almost anything – cheese, fish, meat, prawns or vegetables. The queen of *arepas*, the *Reina Pepiada*, was served to me stuffed with a mixture of shredded chicken, guacamole and mayonnaise.

It was delicious, much tastier than it sounds. I learned later that some believe Venezuelans live on *arepas* – there are dedicated fast-food *areparias* all over the place, and people have them for breakfast, lunch and/or dinner.

WEEK 2 - DAY 1
A BLAZING START TO A DAY IN VENEZUELA

I was only going to be in Venezuela for a little over 24 hours, and I woke up already regretting rushing this trip and trying to be so efficient. I hadn't thought of doing any sightseeing when I'd planned everything. It was such a short time, and I wouldn't even be able to scratch the surface of a country I'd never visited before. I wouldn't even glimpse the capital, Caracas, on this visit.

Within the first few hours of the day, however, I'd changed my mind and was glad to be getting out of Venezuela so quickly.

It started peacefully and routinely, and I was bathed, breakfasted, packed and checked out by 8.30, outside on the veranda (yes, the hotel had one) waiting to be picked up. It proved to be a long wait. So long, I thought I must have been forgotten. I asked the reception clerk to call my plant contact. It was OK, there was "a lot of traffic" and a driver would be there soon. "Soon" turned out to be after 11. I was as nervous as I ever got by then – I knew the plant I was visiting was big, that my visit would take time, and I needed to be back at the airport – 100km away – by 6pm. And not a single car or person had arrived at the hotel in the whole of that time. I was just on my own, on the veranda, with nothing to do, and too unsettled even to enjoy the birdsong.

When a car finally rolled up, I didn't immediately realise it was for me. I'd been looking for a taxi or, more likely, a newish car with a factory driver. I hadn't been expecting an ancient Toyota with bashed-up body panels in a variety of colours. A car that had been in the wars. No taxi sign on the roof or the outside. As for the driver, he looked more like a farm worker. "I'm José, one of the company drivers. Sorry, I got held up."

I said something to him about having been looking out for a taxi. "You'll be safer in this," he replied. *Hmmm. Hope the brakes are in better condition than the bodywork…*

"There are some problems in town," José continued. "We're going to go the long way round."

Naïvely, I took "problems in town" to mean something like roadworks. So, we headed out of town. No road signs, no other traffic; we could have been going anywhere. The unnerving thought of kidnap, put out of my mind the previous evening once Miguel, my bodyguard and driver from the airport, had safely deposited me at the hotel, suddenly came back to me.

"We are going to the car plant, right?" I ventured.

"Sure, sure, another ten minutes."

And, shortly thereafter, cresting a hill, he pointed down at the factory. It appeared at least as big as I had expected, though we still seemed to be quite far away. But then, suddenly, he took a sharp turn off the road, so now we were heading away from it…

"Just as well you speak Spanish, in case we get stopped on the road," said José. Now, that hadn't occurred to me either. We hadn't seen many people around, and there hadn't been much traffic on the roads we'd been on – not enough to cause any delays, assuming we were going in the right direction. Which I was once again doubting.

My state of trepidation reduced briefly as we rounded a bend, ducked through an underpass under the road we'd just exited and, climbing to the top of the crest, the factory came back into view. But there were flames leaping into the sky too. Something big was burning, perhaps a kilometre ahead of us.

As we got closer, I could see that it was two blazing buses, creating a barricade across the road. In front of the buses stood a group of men brandishing home-made placards – not that I ever got close enough to read what they said.

"*Mierda*." José screeched to a halt, and reversed to start a three-point turn – of which points two and three never materialised as, looking back, the road from where we'd come was now filled side-to-side by an advancing column of police, some with riot shields, some on horseback, marching towards us.

José decided, quite reasonably in my opinion, that this wasn't a place to be trapped so his passenger could try out his Spanish with the Venezuelan Riot Police. His solution – drive straight ahead at a tangent to the road, across a vast stretch of wasteland.

My original doubts about whether the car would hold together for more than a few minutes resurfaced and grew as we bounced across the scrub at what felt like a breakneck pace (well, there was definitely a risk of breaking a neck or two).

I now understood for the first time why José had thought I'd be safer in a rust bucket. It was much less likely to be stopped – either by the police or highway robbers – than a new, expensive, polished car, and much less likely to contain a rich person (or someone with rich friends, or working for a foreign company) who could be a kidnap or robbery target. Later, I found the same philosophy at other places I visited across South America, and remembered it when renting cars too, always preferring something common and basic, preferably from a local company that hired out older cars.

Amazingly, the rust bucket held together, my neck stayed in one piece and, suffering only from elevated blood pressure, we reached the plant a few minutes later without further incident.

Alfonso, my host at the factory, obviously didn't consider this incident at all unusual. Apparently, the bus drivers were on strike for more pay, better conditions, or something like that.

"Two buses, eh? Good for us, we'll sell two more new ones."

The factory itself wasn't that much different to many of the others I'd previously visited in Brazil or Europe. What marked this visit apart was experiencing the attitudes of the staff I met. You might think that a car assembly worker is a car assembly worker the same the world over – what can be different about clicking parts into place and bolting things together in one country or another one?

But something about the way they worked caught my attention. Care with a capital 'C'. Popping rivets with love. Repetitive tasks performed with passion. An attitude, seemingly across the whole workforce, that made me think that I'd rather buy a car assembled in Valencia than an identical model made in any other factory in any other country in the world.

I told Alfonso what I was thinking.

"They care about their jobs because none of them can afford to lose them. If any of us leave, we'll never get a job again."

"Really?" I asked. "I was told that the situation in Venezuela was much better now with the new government."

"It's only better for the *politicos* and the *funcionarios*," he replied. "More than half of the rest of us are out of a job, and nobody's hiring any more. Maybe if the Americans can get rid of Chavez," he mused. That was just the first sign that although Alfonso considered himself a working man, he was no socialist. Indeed, quite the opposite.

"Do you think they will?" I asked.

He managed a combination of a shrug and a nod at the same time. "Better we don't talk about it," he said. "Dangerous talk… it costs lives."

Whilst the work attitude on the shop floor had impressed me, I was quickly depressed by my short time in the offices. I hadn't had much previous experience of offices in Latin America – to be honest, only the ones in Brazil a few days before. Those had been quite unremarkable, with a busy and informal atmosphere, although as I understood little Portuguese, I may have been mistaken. Here, everything was very formal. My Spanish was far from perfect, but adequate enough to understand what was going on and to catch the nuances.

Formality, hierarchy and institutionalised misogyny. It had been at least twenty years since I'd been in offices where people who worked together every day called each other 'Mister This' and 'Miss That'. Or, rather, '*Señor Esto y Señorita Esta*'. When I'd gone to work for an American company in London in 1979, there had been signs in the lifts saying, "there are no 'Misters' in this company", to ensure everyone remembered to ditch old-fashioned English formality, and I'd just been plain Oliver to everyone thenceforth, even when I visited less modern-minded companies that were still using titles. I'm pretty sure that by the late 80s titles had disappeared completely, at least in the UK and USA.

Here in Valencia Venezuela, though, in 2002, not only were there titles, but there were engraved name plates on every desk. Gold-coloured for the bosses, silver for middle managers and black for the *hoi polloi*.

It went further. Perhaps it was an architectural accident, and they'd simply adapted to the way the office building was constructed, but I like to think it was deliberately planned. At first sight, the office was unremarkable. Modern and open plan, with closed glass cubes along one side – unsurprisingly the domain of senior management, as tends to be the case the world over. About a third of the open plan area outside, though, was on a raised stage, about 20cm higher than the main floor. The middle managers sat on this stage.

The worker bees were, therefore, literally the lowest in every sense.

Between them and their bosses on the stage was a walkway, with a row of seats that looked exactly like they'd been bought up second-hand from a cinema or theatre. Folding seats in faded red velour. They looked totally out of place.

The only reason I'd come into the office area was to finalise arrangements to have someone send us those copy bills that we needed every month. Alfonso, the plant engineer who had shown me round the factory and identified the energy supplies for me, told me he was not authorised to go into the office building, so he left me outside the entrance. Inside, I was greeted by a charming lady who introduced herself as Señorita Gonzalez, who said she thought she would be sending me the bills, but that this would need to be approved by her boss Señor Garcia first, so would I kindly take a seat and wait for him to become free?

I perched on my cinema seat and watched the office in 3D Panavision and surround sound while I waited. Señorita Gonzalez went and sat at her workstation, just a metre or two away. She picked up her phone and dialled, and I immediately heard a phone ringing behind me. Twisting my head, a quick glance at the name plate on that desk was enough to show me that it was likely this was the guy I was here to see – although I supposed there could have been other Señor Garcias, since it's a very common name. He replaced the receiver. So did the assistant. Proof. She got up and came over to me.

"I'm sorry, but he's terribly busy at the moment, so you will have to wait 10 or 15 minutes." I didn't mind. Despite my late arrival, the plant visit itself had been quicker than I'd expected, and now I didn't need to leave for another hour at least. I kept sneaking looks at Señor Garcia. He ignored me.

But he did spend 10 minutes occasionally moving a piece of paper from one side of his desk to the other, and back again, without looking at it much, and definitely not reading it. Well, that was boring. But the waiting time also gave me the opportunity to watch the rest of a Venezuelan office at work. Watching made easy, as there were no screens between the desks, and only the tiniest computer monitors on them.

As far as I could see from my vantage point, all the bosses were male, and all the lowly office workers were female. I may not have approved, but I wasn't surprised; nevertheless, sitting on one of those cinema seats, it added to the impression that I was watching a live version of a Venezuelan office-based sitcom. All the women wore a uniform of matching blouses and skirts. (Actually, wearing uniform is common to this day for both males and females in many offices in South America, as apparently, so I am told, staff actually prefer it – perhaps as much as anything because it's free clothing provided by the company).

It was quiet. Nobody talked. Only rarely did people move. Everyone communicated with each other by phone. I reached the conclusion that the only reason anyone in the lower level could leave their desk was if they had been instructed over the phone to do so. I was guessing that every (male) manager had a (female) assistant to themselves, as the rough headcount numbers stacked up that way, and most of the women didn't seem to have anything to do apart from wait for a call, then get up and go to a manager's desk, always, in either direction, carrying a folder.

Eventually, Señor Garcia tired of alternately moving his piece of paper across his desk and staring into space, so he picked up his phone. As expected, Señorita Gonzalez picked up hers, and a few moments later, came over and ushered me the five-metre distance to his desk.

"I'm sorry I kept you waiting, I've been so busy, and I didn't see you there."

Hmmm. I introduced myself, made a little small talk, explained why I was there and the need to have copy bills sent to our office every month.

"But of course. Let me think of the best person to arrange that for you." He raised his eyes towards the ceiling, pondering the options (or possibly admiring the light fitting) for a few moments.

"Señorita Gonzalez is the right person. I will instruct her to do this for you." The same Señorita Gonzalez that had showed me to his desk, his assistant. He picked up the phone and called her back. "Please wait here, she will be a few minutes." I attempted some small talk while waiting. He ignored me. In all the other plants I visited, although I craved no special treatment, I tended to be treated as a visiting foreign VIP. Here too, by everyone I met except him. But then, he was far too busy. A very busy man.

Apparently forgetting I was sitting there, he went back to studying the piece of paper he had been moving back and forth around his desk. A spreadsheet. I have no idea what was on it, but it dawned on me that he simply didn't understand it – and presumably felt he needed to.

This thoughtful analysis was interrupted, indeed after only a few minutes, by his assistant, bearing a large dark leather folder, opening and presenting it to Señor Garcia with a flourish and a pen. Inside, three copies of a single sheet, with, on it, a single paragraph and lines for signatures. He read it carefully. He read it again. He then spun it round and pushed it at me. "You need to sign here," he said, pointing at one of the signature lines headed 'Requestor'.

The page was a formal authorisation for Srta Gonzalez to make copies of bills and send them to our office. I'd never seen an authorisation document like this before. It seemed rather an extreme measure just to arrange two or three copies of bills every month. To add to the bureaucratic scenario, if such a thing is possible in South America, the document was even headed with a rather complicated looking 'Instruction Number'.

Well, if that's what it took, no problem. I signed. All three copies. Señor Garcia signed as the 'Authorisor', and finally Señorita Gonzalez herself had to sign as 'Acceptor'. And then – I suppose I should have been expecting this – a drawer was opened, a rubber stamp produced, flourished, inked and duly applied to each copy.

As the señorita took me back to the office building reception, I told her that I'd never seen that before. She smiled. "Here, everything that I do has to have an Authorisation. Every month I have to prepare a sheet for Señor Garcia listing all the Authorisation Numbers, with the date and time when I completed each one and how long it took me."

It seemed ludicrous at the time, but I have to admit that after that, we could always count on getting those bills on the same day every month from her, without fail. Sadly, that wasn't true of other factories; we were always chasing one or another. I hate bureaucracy, and it just seemed so exaggerated; I suppose that, long ago, most offices used to be run like that. It still makes me uncomfortable to think of Señorita Garcia (she wouldn't tell me her first name), a graduate with a qualification in accountancy, and the only job she could get involved working under those conditions for a rather sour, self-important and unpleasant little man who clearly couldn't understand a simple spreadsheet.

Alfonso was waiting for me outside the admin building, taking advantage of the opportunity to smoke.

"Sorry I took so long," I said. "Señor Garcia kept me waiting and there was a surprising amount of bureaucracy."

"Ha," he harrumphed. "I'm not surprised. Garcia is a *politico*. He's on the Central Committee. Spends all his time telling everyone how important he is. His secretary has to serve him his lunch on a separate table in the refectory." I almost expected him to continue with something like "come the revolution…" but then, this was the revolution. *Plus ça change.*

My business for the day finished, we walked to the main gate, where Miguel, the driver I'd had the previous day for the journey from the airport, was waiting for me, this time opening the door to a big, new, shiny black 4x4 with blacked-out windows.

"Armoured car today, you'll be safe in this."

"Is that because of the incident this morning?" I asked.

"What incident? No, I know nothing about any incident."

"OK, but I thought the idea was to be unobtrusive, and blend into the traffic?" I said.

"Normally, yes, but I've got to pick up a visitor from the American company tonight," replied Miguel.

"But I'm a visitor from the company. You didn't pick me up in this car yesterday."

"You're not American. Americans insist on the armoured car. They're scared. They think Venezuela is unsafe."

I think he was expecting me to agree it was safe enough. After my morning experience, I wasn't so sure. "It looks risky to me," I ventured.

"It is much better than it was, and improving every day," enthused my driver. "Everyone is happy now. *Viva la revolución!*". He and Alfonso would have got on like a house on fire. Well – had a flaming row.

A SIDE NOTE ON A LATER VISIT TO VENEZUELA

Two years later, I returned to Venezuela for a follow-up visit to the same factory. Thinking back on my previous experience, I'd come to the conclusion that, in actuality, it was safe enough; I might have *seen* scary things, but nothing had directly affected me other than to drive up my blood pressure for a short time. I'd arrived, stayed, done my job and left; all was good.

This time around, Venezuela was going to be my first stop in South America, coming from Europe. I'd planned another multi-stop trip over two or three weeks, and had all my travel plans arranged when, just two days before I was due to leave London, I got an urgent email from Alfonso at the factory. He would be happy to see me, but this time it was impossible to get anyone to pick me up from Caracas airport; the road was too dangerous and none of their drivers would make the trip. Valencia itself was peaceful, he said, if I could fly into there instead.

The wise thing for me to do would have been to forget going there at all, and re-book to fly from London to my second destination. But I wasn't being wise. In fact, the enforced need to change plans gave me some sort of grim determination to make it there somehow, and my inner travel agent self was challenged by wanting to find a way to fly to Valencia; not a city with any direct flights to anywhere in Europe, and quite probably one that few airlines, if any, would ever have chosen to schedule, even in those days.

I did find a way.

It involved flying KLM via Amsterdam to Curacao, which was exciting in itself because that meant I could visit another unfamiliar country. Now there's something worth leaving home on Saturday morning for! After a night and a day on the island, I could catch a flight with a Venezuelan budget airline to Valencia. I could even book and pay for the flight online, quite a novelty in 2002, and, after checking with my friend at the factory that there would be no problem picking me up from that flight, that's what I did.

Before I got to the airport, I'd been wondering who, if anyone other than me, would want to fly between Curaçao and Valencia. The plane was packed, though, with Venezuelan holidaymakers all returning home. Or perhaps, like so many South Americans taking flights home from other countries, they only went to Curaçao to shop; compared to the mass of packages being checked in by others, my roll-aboard was miniscule.

So, no problems with the flights; a nice visit to a Dutch Caribbean island with pretty coloured houses, a good hotel and a gorgeous beach, then just a raised eyebrow at Valencia immigration, where they had to hunt around in a drawer for the entry stamp, as it was clear they hadn't been expecting any foreigners. The driver was waiting for me; my trusty cross-country battered taxi driver from last time, José, his 'taxi' now sporting a new but old passenger door in a completely different colour to the rest of the car. José and his Amazing Technicolour Taxi.

José told me things were much worse for everyone now, but not to worry, there was no trouble in Valencia. No other foreign visitors were coming, though; he told me I was the first for a year, and I was brave, never something reassuring to hear. On my first visit, the hotel had been quiet; now it was like a morgue. There was at least one other guest, a very quiet older man I found sitting at the other end of the bar when I went for a drink. I greeted him with a "good evening"; in response, he just buried himself in his newspaper. Sitting and watching him, I got to imagining that he was a secret service agent, sent to spy on me; perhaps he was.

My friendly driver picked me up in the morning, this time early and without a hitch. When it came to leaving in the afternoon José simply didn't appear. That got me worried. I had a flight out in the late afternoon. It was the only flight of the day to anywhere, it was going where I wanted to go, and I needed to be on it. A call or two by Alfonso established that José wasn't coming, as he had been arrested. For what or why, I never knew. All I do know is that the plant manager himself took me outside to the gate, waved down a passing police open-top jeep, greased the palm of the officer who was driving, and pushed me into the back next to a man dressed in camouflage with an automatic rifle on his lap. Sirens blaring, I was driven to the airport, scared out of my skin.

The flight left on time, and I lived to tell my tale. That was my last visit to Venezuela, though I still hope to go back sometime, as a tourist, and when the country is more welcoming to foreigners.

In 2017, the factory was ransacked by demonstrators and soon after closed. I do not know how the factory ranked for productivity or profitability before that, but, thinking of the attention to care of the workers and their dedication and determination to keep their jobs, I shed a tear.

WEEK 2 - DAY 2
SAFE AND SOUND IN BOGOTÁ, COLOMBIA

In one sense, I felt angry with myself, having not allowed at least one spare day in Venezuela, if only to visit Caracas. However, my brief experience was enough to realise it wouldn't have been a good idea to wander around on my own, standing out so obviously as a foreigner with my very white skin and (what little remained of it) fair hair.

But then, my next stop wasn't a place most others thought of as safe either. In fact, Bogotá was widely considered not only as less safe than Caracas, but arguably the dangerous capital of the most dangerous country in South America. In terms of gut reaction, the general attitude of most Europeans and North Americans probably has changed little since. But this would not be my first visit; I'd been before, six years earlier in 1996, as a tourist, and had enjoyed my holiday. I felt safe enough returning now.

But allow me to deviate for a few pages and tell you about that earlier holiday.

Those were the days when the FARC guerrillas were at their most active, and the infamy of the Colombian drug cartels was at its zenith – and therefore not a time when most normal people would contemplate a vacation there. So, in the absence of any death wish, why on earth did I go?

Long before then, my wife and I had established a routine whereby we would always go away for a long-haul vacation over Christmas and New Year. As neither of us came from families that treated either festival as a big event, we had no reason to stay at home. We loved travelling and visiting fresh places.

For me, running my own company, it was an ideal time for a holiday. By mid-December, whatever business issue was a crisis at 9am was forgotten by noon, and even before Christmas Eve, all our customers had more or less shut down for the remainder of the year. That meant there was very little chance I'd need to receive or make any urgent phone calls (no email or mobile roaming then). Best of all, it was great to escape the Northern winter for a few weeks of sun in more southerly latitudes.

However, I was never 100% confident of the business situation. Ours was a complicated business providing individually customised services to some of the world's biggest multinational companies, and things went wrong all the time. Mostly, I was the one who had to fix them, so I didn't want to leave festering any crises that I'd have to come back to, in case they gave me nightmares while away and spoiled any chance of relaxation. That meant leaving booking the holiday until quite late. Being a busy season for long-haul flights, with countless people visiting friends and relatives and students and expats going home, all of whom can, and do, book well in advance, by October it can be difficult to get flights to any destination, especially if you have the additional constraint of not being willing or able to pay top dollar.

In the year we went to Colombia, I'd been more paranoid than usual about something, and left booking until November. However, obviously nobody else who wanted to get away had my concerns, as when I came to book, literally all the flights to every destination we had an interest in going to were fully booked. We tried lots of different destinations.

Despite thinking of many places to go, and talking with many friendly agents at several airlines, by mid-November we found ourselves with nothing booked, and starting to get depressed, thinking we'd have to stay at home. But then we read a story in the paper about Colombia – no doubt about drugs, violence, civil war or all three. The article mentioned that its tourism sector, that had been growing fast a decade earlier, was now suffering particularly badly. Ah ha, we thought. We'd been enthusiastic about our previous visits to other countries in South America. Bogotá and Cartagena are renowned as interesting and historic cities. We speak Spanish. The civil unrest seemed to be isolated to just one part of the country, so as long as we avoided that area, we assumed we should be fine. But could we get there?

I phoned Avianca, the national airline. Another friendly agent. So friendly and chatty, in fact, I could have been her only customer in the whole day. Perhaps I was. She told me she was Colombian, and that she was always so happy to talk to people who were going to her country on holiday.

From the way she talked, it didn't sound like there were many of them.

This time it wasn't a case of searching for available dates, but more a case of "when would you like to go?" She even offered a ticket that included a few domestic flights to hop around the country at no extra charge. Less than a month later, we were on a half-empty plane from Paris to Bogotá, upgraded, being treated like royalty (I still remember it as being the first time in my life I was served Beluga caviar) and thinking it was the best airline we'd ever travelled on.

Perhaps it was a deliberate policy that the crew only gave out newspapers after take-off. Yesterday's edition of *El Espectador*. "Less than 100 assassinations in Bogotá yesterday!" screamed the headline. Good news indeed! Things are getting better! Got to have the glass half full attitude! Especially in First Class after a couple of glasses of champagne! Now about that glass half full...

The flight was a great start to an excellent holiday; one that was not without its dodgy moments, though I now think they helped me understand South America better – and to be more prepared for unexpected incidents like those blazing buses in Venezuela.

The plane landed in Santa Fé de Bogotá (to give it its full name) in the late afternoon, and we proceeded through immigration, got a regular taxi and checked in to our hotel. All normal so far. Nothing at all to suggest that this city was any more dangerous than any other capital in the world. The hotel they had advised me to book proved to be pretty basic, though. We wanted a drink and something to eat, but the hotel bar and restaurant were deserted – and would probably have felt pretty uninviting even if they'd been busy. However, we could see the bright lights of a restaurant just across the road, and that did look busy.

Walking out of the hotel, the doorman asked if we wanted a taxi.

"No, we're just going to the restaurant across the road."

"You'll have to take a taxi," he said.

"No – that one, the one with the lights, just across the road."

"Sorry, hotel policy. It is too dangerous at night to cross the road."

Hence the surreal experience of getting into a taxi that simply did a U-turn and deposited us on the opposite side of the road, where an armed doorman came out, scoured the landscape and ushered us in.

But they let us walk back all by ourselves, and we survived crossing the road. The following day, we walked all around the historic centre of Bogotá, with nothing worse than a few mutterings of "*gringo*" by some; there's no way I can blend into a crowd of Latin Americans, not even in Argentina where almost all are of European lineage with relatively few "*indianos*" and "*mestizos*". Back then, in 1996, we were the only foreign visitors that morning in the famous Gold Museum, full of amazing Inca jewellery and art. When I visited it again in 2018, there was a queue round the block to get in.

We spent a happy fortnight after that, travelling around Colombia, welcomed in every hotel and bar as foreign tourists, and constantly being told to tell others to come. Only on a couple of days did we worry that we were in the wrong place at the wrong time.

We'd rented a car in Cartagena to drive to a historic town that we'd been recommended to visit: Mompox. It's a UNESCO cultural heritage site. Reading about it, it seemed impressive; however, we found it to be a fairly small and largely deserted village in the heart of the jungle, so after driving 300km on poor roads, the reality was something of an anti-climax.

To be fair, we hadn't been expecting good roads, but nor had we expected the journey to be so slow. We'd therefore had to make an overnight stop in the only reasonably big town we came across, Santa Ana. A rather impoverished place, but it did have a 'hotel'. Just the one. Unsurprisingly, there was no problem with getting a room, or, should I say more accurately, a cell. It was about 3 metres square, with plain concrete walls, once upon a time painted white, with a mattress on the floor. No bedstead, no furniture. No window; just a foot-high opening running the length of one wall, high up and just below the ceiling. Enough to admit a little daylight by day and faint streetlight by night. And a lot of noises. Weird noises. All quite unsettling when there is no window to see where they might emanate from.

I don't suppose the hotel had many guests who were tourists, and even fewer who were foreigners. Quite possibly, we were the first. If we hadn't already guessed that their principal business was renting rooms by the hour, we soon woke up to it. Lots of bonks in the night and, worryingly, lots of other strange noises from the street outside too.

We'd left the car in a locked yard behind the hotel, guarded, or perhaps better put, watched, by a very dodgy-looking individual. No doubt my imagination was running riot, but some of the noises in the night had sounded like a car being broken into and started. So, with a sense of minor paranoia, and in the absence of a gourmet buffet breakfast in the hotel – or, for that matter, any breakfast at all – we were up and out much earlier than usual.

The car was safe, now being watched over by a small boy, so we relaxed enough to grab a disgusting coffee from a bar. Why is it that countries that grow coffee beans serve such a horrible brew? Colombia, Brazil, Ethiopia, Kenya… all are famous for the coffee they grow, but I don't remember having a great brew in any of them.

The rest of the drive from Santa Ana was unremarkable. Mompox is a little town but boasted several hotels – all pretty basic, 'normal' hotels aimed at tourists, but not getting many. We dedicated an entire hour to seeing the sights – at least 20 minutes more than strictly necessary. That gave us lots of time to study the map and plan our escape. Surely we didn't have to go back the same way? No, the map showed another road back to Cartagena through what looked like a lake district. We inquired at reception, and were told that yes, it was possible to go that way. Maybe I should have noted the raised eyebrows and asked more questions.

The road started well, but after just a few kilometres came to an end. At a river. No signs, no buildings, nothing, just a river. And a man, standing there, with a goat tethered with a rope. "The ferry's coming soon," he volunteered. The map indicated nothing about a ferry.

Well, ferry. For which, read raft. Looking rather like – and just as safe as – an oversized pallet, crewed by a wizened man hauling on a rope stretched shore to shore. With considerable misgivings, I drove the car onto the raft, followed by the man and goat, both of whom stood calmly, clearly regular sailors.

The road started again on the other side, but now it was just a dirt track. We crossed our fingers, hoping that it wouldn't be far before it got back to being asphalt. In fact, it stayed as a dirt track all the way to the next town. A dirt track running in a straight line through the forest, for more than 100km. No visible habitation. Not one other car or truck passed or overtaken. Over three hours of a bumpy and dusty ride in a rental car that had once seen much better days – several years previously – and that probably didn't have a usable – or in fact any – spare tyre.

If we'd had an incentive to stop on that road – whether to check the spare or some other reason – that disappeared completely after we'd driven the first 20km or so. Suddenly, ahead of us, a group of men ran out of the forest and pulled a thick rope across the road. There was no time to look at them properly, but they didn't look friendly. I still don't know why, but my reflex reaction was to foot the accelerator and drive straight through – never a good idea on a dirt track, except perhaps for rally drivers. I'm not sure who was more surprised, me or them, but I found myself looking in the rear-view mirror and seeing men lying on the road, I suppose pulled down by the force of the rope.

We contented ourselves for the rest of the journey thinking that they were most likely just kids who wanted to get money. Recounting the story to the stunned receptionist in the hotel we checked into in the next town, we were told in a very serious tone that we'd been very, very lucky. "They didn't shoot?" she asked, sounding amazed.

Looking back at the history of conflict now, I suppose I should have been more careful. The FARC uprising lasted for over 30 years and was only officially resolved in 2016 with a peace agreement – that being said, it still rumbles on a little. Nearly 200,000 civilians were killed, including around 20,000 in the year that we visited; not only in the coca-growing areas to which I had believed the violence was limited, but over around 20% of the country.

Maybe I didn't want to be told that it was dangerous; I didn't want to be put off travelling. After I returned from the 2002 trip, I finally read up on Colombian kidnapping, expecting the risks to have been exaggerated. But no. By 2000, the various guerrillas were using the extortion that comes with kidnapping to finance their operations; they were reportedly kidnapping more than 10 people a day, mostly Colombian politicians or business people. But the number included around 80 foreigners a year, people working for big corporations, a number assumed to be a big underestimate as companies and insurers were reluctant to admit the truth. I shouldn't have been surprised that my contacts were paranoid enough to collect me from the airport and send me back in an armoured car.

And now, to return to my business trip…

Anyway, having not only survived but enjoyed a fortnight in Colombia at the height of the troubles, and with those interesting experiences in my anecdotal bag, I had no qualms about arriving in Bogotá, especially now things seemed to be – temporarily, as it turned out – a bit calmer. A new President, Alvaro Uribe, had just been elected on a platform that he was going to get FARC defeated and restore external confidence in the country. He was a man on a mission – FARC guerrillas had assassinated his own father.

This time, *El Tiempo*, the daily newspaper they gave me on the plane from Caracas, was full of news of big military mobilisations and expectations of some sort of peace deal being struck. At least there was no front page news about assassination statistics. Certainly nothing to raise concerns.

However, after my Venezuelan experience, I wasn't in the least surprised to be met at the airport by a uniformed armed escort, who introduced himself as Jorge. Over the top? Walking from the arrivals hall to the car park didn't give me the impression that a lot of security was necessary or, that if an attempt was made to kidnap me, Jorge, who was short and bulky and didn't look like someone who could run fast, would have been much use at preventing it. I'm not sure he would even have noticed any attacker creeping up; he talked non stop, accompanied by expansive hand gestures. It would surely have been little effort for a young and agile villain to nip past and grab his gun from his belt, and maybe grab me at the same time.

It also struck me that having a uniformed armed escort marked me out as a potential hostage of value. But I wasn't nervous, and was reassured anyway by Jorge's exuberant explanations of how things had got so much better in the last year, "although there are always local kids in my *barrio* fighting and sometimes shooting each other, but that's nothing to do with FARC, just boys will be boys…"

His car was big, black, and armoured. An enormous one, even bigger than the one in Venezuela. I'm reminded of those airport transfers every time I see the US president on TV being chauffeured somewhere in 'The Beast'. I guess those trips will be the nearest I ever get to being presidential, at least in terms of transport.

Jorge's entertaining descriptions of life in modern-day Colombia went on non-stop until we reached my hotel, modern and nondescript from the outside, but posher inside than I expected from a middle-of-the-range chain. Apart, that is, from the restaurant, which looked like a purely functional works canteen with bright red plastic tables and chairs. It was empty, perhaps because the hotel wasn't busy, but just as likely because the menu was as unappetising as the ambience. I was starving, and wanted my favourite Colombian dish, *ajiaco* – I'd been looking forward to that all afternoon.

Ajiaco is a 'meal in a soup'. Or, maybe, 'soup as a meal'. I cook it myself sometimes, at least as close as I can get to it (you can find my recipe on my website *www.oliverdowson.com*). It's difficult to replicate the dish outside Colombia because of the difficulty of matching some of the ingredients. That might strike one as surprising, as the key ingredients are potatoes. But not the varieties you usually see here. Three different sorts of potato are used: *papas criollas*, *sabaneras*, and *tocarreñas*, respectively yellow, red, and white. Each has a different texture, cooks in a different way, and makes its own contribution to the soup.

The other ingredient of magic is the herb, *guascas* – also found in Colombian grocers.

Apart from potatoes, the main cooked ingredients are chicken and corn cobs. The result is a thick potato and chicken soup, which is eaten with lots of sliced avocado, thick cream and capers – oh, and the corn cob. Simple but bewitching. You'd never imagine potatoes could be so delicious.

When I make it at home, try as I might at authenticity, it's never the same. *Ajiaco*'s natural habitat is Bogotá, and that's where it really has to be enjoyed. So, having checked in and dropped my bag in my room, I sought directions from the clerk on the front desk as to the best nearby restaurant for *ajiaco*, and set off in the direction indicated. It was just a short walk away, and this time I didn't get stopped and told to take a taxi.

That may have been because it was still daylight. Later, leaving the restaurant in the dark, I saw more moving shadows than street lights between me and the hotel. The taxi that just happened to be hovering outside made it easy to chicken out of walking back. The driver wasn't in the least fazed by the journey being less than 500 metres. I suppose it was a long journey if he was used to passengers only asking him to take them to the opposite side of the road.

Despite a heavy stomach replete with *ajiaco* I slept soundly, and woke refreshed, ready for my day at the factory. Not seeing the 'beast' armoured car outside, I stood waiting. And waiting. It never came. After Venezuela, I should not have been surprised that my chauffeur would in fact be picking me up in a battered old Toyota saloon, but I spent ten minutes looking at it before the penny dropped.

No burning buses this time; but plenty of open 4x4s on the road, with police or military sitting at the back, rifles at the ready, all evidently having some place to go, in a hurry, and posing no threat to us.

Today's driver, Manolo, assured me that things were getting much better, though he didn't think that I or anyone else should yet be walking down the street without a gun. He seemed rather cynical about whether the calm would last. But the journey to the plant, and later my return back to the airport, proved uneventful.

My day at the factory involved lots of walking – it's a very big site, with many buildings – much helpful discussion with very pleasant and friendly people, willing and useful assistance, plus the standard canteen lunch of rice and beans, of even better quality than in Valencia. I saw very different attitudes to work here; I've always found it fascinating watching and learning how people in different countries function in their places of employment, especially in cases such as this, where they're essentially doing exactly the same things in the one industry. How many ways can there be of bolting a handle onto a car door? Can one judge quality of workmanship simply by watching someone do a routine manual task? Does it make a difference to the finished product if the person who fits that handle is enthusiastic or apathetic?

In the office here in Bogotá, there was no visible hierarchy; more an air of busy efficiency, with lots of meetings going on, making it feel much more like a US office. But down on the factory floor, that sense of dedication I'd detected and assumed in the Venezuelan workforce was absent; more an attitude of "it's a job, I'll do what I need to do to keep it, but no more". That may not be fair, as, just visiting for a few hours, I only got a superficial impression. I may have been wrong about Venezuela. And, anyway, do first impressions really count for much of anything that can be valued? In this case, genuinely I don't know, but nevertheless, I still found it a fascinating thought, and case for comparison here, there, and in other instances since.

Like every other stop on this South American tour, I got so much more from it than the data I went there for; learning new things, meeting new people and soaking up a little of another culture. What more could one hope for from a business day anywhere in the world?

Looking back on Colombian recent history now, what I had been told about the security situation was rather over-optimistic, and my morning driver's cynicism proved well-placed. A peace deal and the disarmament of FARC finally came to pass in 2016, and even then only after many failed attempts. Occasional isolated insurrections continue to be reported, so perhaps the violence and danger is still not over.

WEEK 2 - DAY 3
FLYING SCARED INTO QUITO, ECUADOR

Another day, another airport. Bogotá. A perfectly functional and entirely forgettable airport. Except for a foreigner like me, with a ticket to Quito on an airline I had never previously heard of, and that sounded a bit suspicious – TAME. Not tame as in harmless, but 'Transportes Aereos Militares de Ecuador' – Ecuadorian Military Air Transport. Sure, Avianca flew the route, but not at a time that worked for my ridiculous schedule. Crazy me needed to fly in the evening. Even if that meant joining a bunch of soldiers sitting on the floor of a Hercules (though I hoped for something more comfortable).

I got dropped off at the airport around 6pm, and looked for the right check-in desk. There were lots, mostly for Avianca, but not one that I could see for TAME. More concerning, the flight wasn't listed on the departures board – there were lots beforehand and a few later, but not mine. No other flights to Quito either. What was I going to do now?

The harassed-looking individual on the airport information desk denied all knowledge of the flight. "If it's not on the board, it's not going." And denied all knowledge of the airline. "Never heard of it. Ask Avianca."

Although I found many charming Avianca agents, none knew anything about TAME either. Nor did the check-in agents for other airlines. Now quite wound up, thinking that I had a worthless ticket, no flight until the next day (and even then, assuming it had seats) and a screwed-up schedule, I asked a passing heavily armed policeman. In retrospect, it would have been a good idea to start with him. I should have listened to my mother; "when in doubt, always ask a policeman". Even when he presents like an assassin with a machine gun slung round his neck.

Not only had he heard of TAME, but he also knew that the flight existed, and could even tell me how to check in for it. "Stand over there at the far end of the check-in desks, she'll turn up about 8pm." OK, though getting a bit tight as the flight is at 9pm, if it's on time that is – or exists at all.

8 o'clock came and went. One other man arrived; he looked Ecuadorian, if there is such a stereotype, in that he was dressed in a stripy poncho, with pan pipes hanging around his neck on a red and yellow rope, and sporting a wide-brimmed leather hat. Incongruously, he was also carrying a big backpack. He looked like he was waiting, too. I asked, and indeed he was waiting for the same flight. "It's past 8.30, the flight's in less than half an hour," I said. "Maybe it's cancelled?" "Oh, don't worry, they go when they feel like it," replied my pan-piper.

How did I ever end up in this situation?

I'd found the flight on an online system I liked to use, EasySABRE. It appealed to my inner travel agent to arrange all my own itinerary. Usually, in those days, I bought tickets directly from airlines, paying by card over the phone. But there was no TAME office outside Ecuador. So, I'd had to buy my ticket through a travel agent.

I'd done that in London before I left. The agent hadn't heard of TAME either, but found the flight on Amadeus (like Sabre, another of the major global airline reservation systems), succeeded in making a reservation on it, printed me out a ticket, took my money and wished me good luck... ominously.

A few minutes later, a very short woman carrying a very big bag arrived. Opening the bag, she extracted a board and held it proudly above her head. It simply said 'QUITO'. A few other would-be passengers that I hadn't spotted before trickled across from odd corners of the terminal where they'd been lurking. I handed over my ticket, and in return was given a tattered – if plastic can be tattered – boarding pass, on which she wrote the number '2' with a felt-tip pen (Pan-Piper was number 1). "Go to gate now! No checked bags, take everything with you!"

Still no sign of the flight on the Departures board. Never mind, I had my pass... and I was not alone! At the gate, I counted seven of us. It was already past 9pm, but no plane was parked at the gate. The monitor above the gate that should be showing the relevant airline and flight number was switched off. But there's strength in numbers, and if I've got a lucky number, it's seven.

Ten nervy minutes later and, simultaneously, I could see through the window a plane pulling into the gate, and the check-in lady reappearing. I assumed it wouldn't take long to board. There were no seat numbers, but who cares when there are only seven passengers?

In fact, boarding took longer than I'd expected. First, someone at the front of the queue didn't seem to have the right documentation and got engaged in a heated argument with a policeman, the check-in lady and a man who looked like (and presumably was) a pilot. Then there was the quantity of luggage the other passengers had with them. My little wheely case and Pan-Piper's backpack looked insignificant by comparison. How the other passengers had got the number of cardboard boxes and cabin trunks that they'd brought with them through security and as far as the gate beat me.

Too big for overhead lockers, all those boxes and bags had to go on seats. In the end, I'm sure there must have been more seats occupied by baggage than people.

The plane was not a military Hercules, thank goodness. It was a 727. Inside, it didn't look very well cared for, but it was already at least half an hour after scheduled departure time, it had been quite an experience getting this far, and frankly I was just happy to sit down on a plane that was going where I wanted to go.

Taxi, hold, take off. Not just the aircraft. Boxes and bags also took off from the seats they'd been left on, some, impressively, sliding all the way down the aisle from front to rear as the plane climbed. At least I was strapped in. The cabin crew – more than seven of them, so more than the collective number of passengers – calmly picked up and repositioned the boxes; obviously they were used to this happening. Then, once the plane had reached cruising altitude, they handed out the inflight magazine.

Such as it was. Two sheets of paper, photocopies, stapled together. Dog-eared. "Please leave on plane for the next passenger." You have been warned.

Other than the format, the only memorable thing about it was the introduction on the front page. "TAME proudly flies the oldest Boeing 727 in commercial service today." They didn't add "and to keep it authentic we haven't spent a cent on internal maintenance since it was built"; I suppose they expected passengers to reach that conclusion for themselves. As I leant gently back and my seat collapsed, I crossed my fingers and hoped that the mechanical maintenance was better. Well, we'd taken off, and were on our way. Just a couple of hours to go.

Bogotá is a high Andean city, but Quito is higher still. Only La Paz in Bolivia is higher. One common characteristic of high Andean cities is that they have frequent night-time electrical storms. That night was one such time and, as the plane started to descend towards Quito, the sky lit up with spectacular jagged bolts of lightning.

I'd flown through storms a few times before, so it didn't worry me much at first. The plane tossed and yawed a bit, gently at first, then more violently. I heard a passenger behind me cry out. That always happens with strong turbulence. So far, though, it didn't feel like the worst I'd experienced.

I could feel the plane continuing to descend; no smooth glide, though, it felt more like going down stairs, tripping step by step, swaying side to side, as if in an alcoholic stupor. "Five minutes to landing," came the announcement. Then it hit. The lightning hit. Or, at least, that's what I assumed happened – there was an almighty bang, a short, sharp, very loud crack, the plane tossed this way and that, and all the lights went out…

This time, there were screams from the back of the cabin. I'm sure I screamed myself. I can remember the blind panic to this day. I honestly thought my time had come.

But then, like a miracle, I felt the familiar thud as the plane landed and the screech of the engines as they went into reverse thrust. The runway seemed to go on forever, but at last we stopped. A landing. Maybe not a safe one, but we were on the ground – and alive.

I couldn't see a thing, either in the plane or outside. The cabin crew came to life, coming down the aisle waving torches. Not to help me and the other passengers get off the plane; no, they had a much more critical task to perform, retrieving the copies of the inflight magazine that they'd given out after take-off. Making sure the evidence didn't leave the scene of the crime.

Now, through the window, I could see trucks and vans with lights, and could hear a lot of shouting going on. I was experiencing an inner desperation to get off the plane – somehow I was now nervous that something terrible would happen – but it was reassuring to see some signs of normality outside as it was pitch black inside, apart from the crew's torches.

Eventually, I descended the steps from the plane, and realised then that we'd stopped at what must have been the far end of the runway. The lights of the terminal looked far away. At least the storm was over. Looking back at the plane, I saw men up ladders at the cockpit, now floodlit, pulling out shards of broken glass and dropping them to the ground. I suppose a window had been broken by the lightning; I thought that those on a plane were all made of plastic, but it definitely sounded like broken glass being dropped. Pan-Piper and I, the first down the steps with our light luggage, could stand and watch while the other passengers and cabin crew struggled down, laden with boxes and bags. Once all those had been loaded, there wasn't any space left in the minibus that turned up to take us to the terminal.

So, a TAME flight, but not a tame flight. More of an experience, really. But I'd made it. By now, it was well past midnight. The terminal was eerily silent; obviously this was the last flight of the day. But there was a uniformed man to greet us as the bus pulled up.

"Bags will be on Carousel 3!" he shouted. *Er, no.*

But I still hadn't legally arrived in Ecuador. Immigration first. I joined the queue for foreigners; all one of me. If I hadn't already worked out that only locals were crazy enough to fly their own airline, it was pretty obvious now. The immigration desk was unmanned. After a while, an officer in military uniform arrived from somewhere. He waved through Pan-Piper and his countrymen and women with just a cursory glance at their ID cards. With nobody else waiting, and no other flights coming, and perhaps with no home to go to, or an eye to overtime, he then decided to give me the third degree.

I've been to Ecuador several times since, and never waited more than seconds in immigration. There's no visa requirement for UK nationals… if, that is, they are just 'visiting'. I wasn't expecting any problems.

But he took his time. Asked where I was coming from, where I was staying, how long, all the usual stuff. Then, he wanted to know if I was travelling on business.

"Si". Fool that I am…

"You do not have a visa."

"I don't need one for a short visit."

"If it's business, you need one."

All in Spanish, of course.

It's never wise to argue with officialdom anywhere, and I had no intention of doing so there and then. But it's difficult, well almost impossible for me, not to get irritable hitting up against intransigent bureaucracy at 1am in the morning, especially after a long day and a not-so-relaxing evening's journey. I was angry with myself, too, for never having checked about needing a visa for business travel, and that added into the mix to make me more nervous.

At least I held my nerve enough to switch to English. First rule of resolving difficult situations in a foreign country: pretend you don't understand or, if like me you speak and understand the language, pretend that you only know a few words.

I'd not expected him to have this capacity – I don't know why – but he spoke perfect English. My adrenalin kicked in enough to give me an idea.

"Sorry I didn't explain myself; I only speak a little Spanish. I was on business in Colombia and I'll be on business in Peru, but I haven't been to Ecuador before and I have to change planes here, so I thought I would spend a day visiting Quito as a tourist."

"Why didn't you get a direct flight to Lima from Bogotá?"

"It was much more expensive, and I wanted to visit Quito."

"So, you are flying TAME again? Really?"

"Yes."

"Hmm, they always say you British are crazy."

And with that, I got my entry stamp. I don't suppose he believed me, and he just wanted to go back to sleep, but he'd performed his actions of officialdom, and could probably write it up somewhere to show his superiors how diligent he had been in the small hours of the morning with a foreigner who aroused his suspicions.

I looked up the rules later. He was wrong, or more to the point, it's a matter of interpretation. You don't need a visa to visit Ecuador (or most other countries in South America) for a business meeting. You only need a business visa if you're going to work and get paid for it, or if you are providing a 'valuable' service (however that might be classified). For years afterwards, I relied on saying, whenever challenged in any country, that I was just visiting for meetings, but I know that often I was pushing the boundaries.

Despite the late hour, there was still a taxi waiting outside the terminal. The driver had obviously been even more pessimistic than me about whether the flight from Bogotá would ever arrive, as I had to wake him up. No armed guards or organised transport here; in Ecuador, supposedly being a relatively safe country, I was back on my own.

And it was no problem. We sped through empty streets and what looked like slums, enough to make me not expect much of the hotel when we got there. Much to my amazement, and considerable delight, though, it was quite splendid and new. The best and most memorable thing about the room was the shower, so desperately needed: they're ubiquitous now, but it was the first time I'd ever seen or experienced a ceiling mounted powered 'rain' shower. In all the world, it was one of the most unlikely cities I could have thought would be premiering such a thing.

Next day, a short city walk round Quito – well, the bit of it near the hotel – after breakfast and before going in to the factory, left me breathless; not from walking fast, but from the altitude. I hadn't noticed at night when I'd arrived, but I did now; even a stroll of a few hundred metres left me panting. I knew I was unfit, but... This despite having just come from Bogotá, another of South America's top-of-the-mountain cities, but where I hadn't noticed the altitude at all. Quito is only a little higher – 2,850 metres compared to Bogotá's 2,644 metres, but I found the effect noticeable. It takes a day or two to acclimatise; something else I should have considered before planning to make this trip at such a breakneck pace.

As a side note, both these cities pale by comparison with La Paz in Bolivia, which at 3,640m is the highest capital in the world. Its airport, El Alto (an appropriate name – it means 'the high one') sits around 400m higher still above it, on the rim of an extinct volcano at 4,061m. I wasn't going there on this trip – it didn't have any of my client's factories – but I had been there before; it's famous amongst travellers for the fact that arriving passengers are met off their aircraft by paramedics with oxygen masks, prepared to cope with anyone fainting on arrival.

The altitude hadn't affected me in La Paz, and it was only a quick 'catch my breath' moment here in Quito. The only time I really noticed and suffered from the altitude was five years later, on a return visit to Quito, this time as a tourist. Then, strolling in the early afternoon around the historic city centre, quite near the Parliament building, I turned into a narrow city street, and immediately discovered it was barricaded a hundred metres or so ahead of me. Not by burning buses like in Venezuela, but by police with riot shields and horses. The intelligent thing to do would have been to turn and go the other way – except that was no longer an option; looking back, I saw I had been followed by a mob of protesters carrying placards.

I'd seen a demonstration parading through the streets earlier in the day, but it was smaller, very peaceful and good-natured. It wasn't obvious what they were protesting about. In fact, that crowd earlier hadn't been protesting about anything – I asked a fellow bystander, who told me that it was a march in favour of the government, with placards saying how wonderfully the president was treating the agricultural community. I found out later that the morning demonstration had been organised entirely by the government. They brought people in from the countryside by bus, and rewarded them for their half-hearted parading round the city centre with a free lunch and a day out in the capital.

The afternoon demo was different. These were real demonstrators. It took me a few minutes to realise this and, while the neurons in my brain were making the necessary connections, I even had enough time to stop and take some photos. As the marchers got nearer, I could read the placards and realised what exactly was occurring; these people had a definite grudge against the government, coming here not to praise it but to attempt to bury it.

I quickly learnt that the Ecuadorian government wasn't prepared to brook any criticism. For the first time in my life, I found myself being the target of tear gas. The marchers ran. I couldn't. I can't run at sea level, even if my life depends on it, and at that altitude, under the effects of gas, I couldn't even stagger for my life. Eyes streaming, panting for air, I lost any sense of what was happening. The effects probably took ten minutes to wear off; when I 'came to', I found myself alone, sitting on the kerb, in what was now a totally deserted street.

Fortunately, this first time, my visit to Quito went off without incident. My early morning walk had revealed a much poorer and more chaotic city than most others I'd visited in Latin America – although perhaps that was just because I had more time to explore, or that I'd stumbled on more downmarket areas. The factory I was visiting was actually in the centre of the city, so I could walk there. Such a location is unusual; most car plants are large sheds sited on big plots of land, either on the edge of town or out in the middle of nowhere. But this one was very different. This 'factory' comprised more than a dozen buildings scattered over adjacent city blocks, with ordinary and busy streets running between them.

Long ago, a small factory had been built to assemble buses. That building was still in use, serving the same purpose. Indeed, the buses I'd seen burning in Valencia may well have been built here in Quito. Now, however, as well as buses, the factory assembled at least a dozen different cars and trucks, more or less made bespoke to order. To accommodate the growth in their business, they'd simply bought up adjacent buildings as years had gone by, and either repurposed them or razed and rebuilt, resulting in what was now described as a 'factory' being spread across a weird higgledy-piggledy collection of buildings. Nevertheless, they'd achieved a surprisingly cohesive operation.

Far from the robotised production lines I'd seen in factories I'd visited in Europe, or the identical but manual assembly process of a single model that I'd seen in Venezuela and Colombia, the approach here looked quite haphazard – different groups of men working on a car here, a 4x4 there, a lorry in one corner and a bus in another. Instead of moving the vehicle being worked on from one set of operators to the next, here it stayed put, and the assembly mechanics moved around instead. Hardly surprising, I suppose, as the spread of buildings made a 'production line' nigh on impossible.

My local contact and guide, Nacho, bore an uncanny resemblance to Pan-Piper from the night before, despite being dressed 'normally', with no poncho or musical instruments hanging around his neck. Nacho's first priority was to introduce me to the entire management team, all of whom seemed thrilled to see me. I'm sure they knew I was no celebrity, but nonetheless I was treated like one. Apparently, it was just that visits from the US parent company, or any other foreign visitors, were rare.

As always on this trip, a key reason for my visits was to identify which electricity, gas and water bill related to which bit of the factory. Unsurprisingly, given the nature of the site, there were lots of bills – at least one electricity and water bill for each building, and sometimes several. Nacho had absolutely no clue which one was which, but set off on our expedition with me with all the enthusiasm of an eight-year-old embarking on a long and particularly tricky treasure trail or Easter Egg hunt. He was also plainly determined to make sure that our search would take all day. Having started by telling me that his shift ended at 5pm, and then finding the first few electricity meters quite quickly, he slowed the tour down to a glacial pace, simply by stopping, introducing me and chatting unnecessarily to anyone he recognised along the way, and only speeding up mid-afternoon when I pointed out that by then we'd only tracked down about half the meters we were looking for.

Many of the meters were in hard-to-reach locations, and my sheaf of papers – photocopies of the latest bills – became progressively dirtier and more dog-eared as I kept shuffling and dropping them (inevitably, it seemed, into oil spills). Any faith that I'd be able to read my own writing later, and work out what bill belonged to which building or process, was diminishing fast.

Nacho was falling over himself to be helpful and make efforts to impress me. If I couldn't already have guessed, his motives became crystal-clear at lunch time.

"Can you get me a job in America?" he asked.

"Sorry, no, I'm not American and I don't work directly for the company."

"I could come and work for your company in England?" he suggested. "I am a very good engineer. I work very hard."

"I'm sure that you are, but we don't need any engineers. We only have offices, not factories." If I'd hoped that would close the subject, I was wrong.

"I can do many things. I can do what you are doing today. I can go to factories and look for meters. You can train me, I would be very good at it."

"I'm sure you would, but we don't need to do this very often. We don't have any jobs for anyone in London." It was true; we did keep employing new people, but not in the UK.

I didn't tell him that, though, as I'm sure he would have then asked for a job in Frankfurt or Chicago or anywhere. A phenomenal number of people in Latin America want to emigrate in the hope of finding a better life. Nacho told me that although he had a good job by Ecuadorian standards, the pay wasn't good enough to bring up his five children properly and his wife was always telling him to get a job in Spain or America. Five children is not an unusually big family in Ecuador.

Fortunately, the fact that I couldn't help him emigrate didn't stop him from doing everything he could to help for the rest of the day.

The real high point came towards the end of the afternoon, when we'd explored every corner of every building, and were left with just one electricity and one water bill that we couldn't tie to any part of the plant. Which was surprising, because unlike most of the others, it actually had a supply address on it. It was getting close to clocking-off time, so Nacho, now moving fast, raced off in search of someone who might be able to help, dragging me in his wake.

That someone was the finance manager. He recognised the address immediately. In Quito, properties have street names and block numbers, but not individual building or door numbers. And the factory did have one of its buildings on that block.

As you may have guessed, another company also had a building on that block and street. It took only minutes after that to prove that the meters and bills belonged to them, but had been paid by the car plant for at least the last 20 years. I know it was only an electricity bill, and quite a small one, but it was an emotional moment; on one side the euphoria of my guide, believing that he could now claim to have unearthed a huge saving for the company, and on the other the embarrassment of the finance manager, who, after all, had been the one responsible for paying those bills that entire time.

So, that wrapped it up. All done by 5pm! Nacho could go home on time, and I, now the proud possessor of a sheaf of dirty and oil-stained bills covered with my scrawls, could look forward to an evening in my luxurious hotel trying to decipher what I'd written and transcribe the important bits to a clean notebook. This reminded me, with irritation, that I was still lugging my burnt-out computer from city to city. It wasn't until I got back to London and sent it for repair that I learnt that I should have simply ditched it where it died.

But first, with my flight not until the following morning, enough time to explore a little of Quito's centre in the fading daylight and find a restaurant to enjoy some Ecuadorian cuisine – and, more urgently, a beer. Thirsty work, this meter-hunting. There are local competitors and many craft breweries now, but back in 2002, Ecuador's only beer was Pilsener (a brand, not a type). Served very cold – maybe not as '*estupidamente gelada*' as in Brazil – it's very refreshing, and much better than its brand ubiquity might suggest. I found a good table on an inviting terrace on the main square, populated by an interesting mixture of men in suits and men in ponchos, all of them involved in raucous conversation, and settled back to people-watch.

There's not much to say about Ecuadorian cuisine. I suppose the national dish is *cuy*, roast guinea pig. Why I was reticent to try guinea pig for many years, when I have no qualms about ordering rabbit when it's on the menu, I don't really know; I didn't keep one as a pet when I was a child, nor remember knowing anyone who did. I did eventually try eating it a few years later – it's like a gamier version of rabbit, I suppose. It may have been that the restaurant I chose it in wasn't very good, but it certainly didn't make me a convert, or encourage me to order it ever again. Once tried…

On this occasion, I had goat – *chivite* – instead, another common national dish, cooked into a fairly dry stew and, like most dishes in the mountains, served with a pile of potatoes. Nourishing, but as far removed from *Masterchef* as it's possible to imagine.

A WEEKEND EXPEDITION
FROM ECUADOR TO CHILE VIA PERU

A sunny Saturday morning. Ah, the weekend! Time to relax and enjoy the sunshine? Of course not. I was on a crazy business trip. So, what to do? In my case, fly from one unlikely location to a much less likely one via yet another. Hours in planes, even more hours in airports. But, as you know by now, I love to travel so much that it seemed like a good idea.

My destination was Arica, a small city in the far north of Chile. It has a busy airport, with almost all the flights from and to Santiago, the Chilean capital. Therefore, almost every airline reservation system routes passengers coming from anywhere in the world via Santiago. But look at the map; coming from Quito, it's geographically absurd. First, the non-stop flight between the two cities actually flies over Arica before landing three hours later in Santiago – and then, after changing planes, one has another three-hour flight back north to Arica. The journey seems at least seven hours longer than necessary.

I'd discovered another connection via La Paz, Bolivia, but in the course of the fortnight between deciding to travel that way and actually leaving London, it had stopped operating. Another of those South American airline failures. I wasn't surprised. Time for Plan B. I searched again, and I found what I thought to be a logical and much more original route, and for a fact one highly unlikely to be found or suggested by any European travel agent (although few, if any, would be likely to have any customer who wanted to go to Arica).

This routing meant flying first to Lima, Peru, and then taking a domestic flight due south to Tacna, a town just north of Peru's southern border with Chile. It's only about 30km from Arica, so I figured I'd be able to find a bus or taxi to take me over the frontier from Tacna to Arica, or maybe just as far as the frontier, where I could walk across and catch another one the other side. I'd emailed asking my contact in Arica whether it was possible to cross from Tacna, and he'd confirmed that it could be done.

So, first stop: Lima. Looking at the timetables, what would have been the least stressful arrangement would have been to take the afternoon flight from Quito to Lima, stay overnight, then catch the first flight the following day to Tacna. That would mean arriving in Lima about 10pm and leaving at 8am the next day. Unfortunately, that wasn't practicable, simply because I couldn't find any hotels in or near the airport in Lima. Not that I was looking in the wrong place – there really weren't any. The nearest hotel was about 15km away and, allowing for the time to get there

109

and back, I'd be lucky to catch five hours of sleep. And no time at all to see Lima or enjoy Peruvian cuisine.

The alternative was to catch an early morning flight from Quito and connect with an afternoon flight from Lima to Tacna. Whilst that made sense, it was risky. There was not much more than an hour between the two flights. I had never been to Lima airport, so didn't know how long the connection might take. I needed two different tickets on two different and unrelated airlines. And, well, this was South America, where nothing can be relied on for running to published timetables.

I'd told the immigration officer in Quito that I would be flying TAME, but I was actually booked on another airline. That wasn't because my one experience had dissuaded me, though if I'd been booked with them for this leg, it might well have done. A few months later, I learnt that the aviation authorities had banned TAME from operating international flights. Not only had others, more influential than me, reported dodgy flying experiences with them, but just a week or two after my experience, one of their flights hadn't reached its intended destination. It hit a volcano. About five years later, I flew with them again, on a domestic flight from Guayaquil to the Galapagos, but by that time they'd bought a new Airbus. Presumably because all the passengers on that route were likely to be foreign tourists.

No, my early morning flight was with TACA instead, a much more reliable airline that was building a reputation for itself. (It's since been taken over by Avianca). The flight was on time and arrived in Lima a few minutes early.

That was just as well for my nerves, as I discovered that domestic flights operated from a different terminal that was quite a long walk away from where I had landed. I arrived at the check-in desk for AeroPeru sweating, puffing and panting, just 30 minutes before departure. But no sweat from the agent. "Go straight to the gate," I was instructed.

Hurry, hurry. At least there was no passport control – and, from what I remember, no credible security screening either. All the gates (well, glass doors) were next to each other on one side of the departure hall, which was pretty basic; a big, tall shed, largely filled with seats and with all the gaps in-between also filled with waiting passengers. Hundreds of them. All with lots and lots of luggage. Nowhere for me to sit.

Never mind, I thought – the departure board showed my 13:00 flight as being on time. I'd only have to wait a few minutes before boarding started.

No longer puffing and panting, I realised that the flight shown on the monitor above Gate 2 was, in fact, not my flight, not even my airline or my destination. And nobody seemed to be queuing up for it. Indeed, none of the hundreds of people sitting or standing around me looked like they were expecting to go anywhere anytime soon.

Taking a more studied look at the departure board, I saw that there were a dozen or more other flights showing with earlier departure times. Was the board not being updated, or were the other flights due to leave up to four hours ago still not boarded? Unsurprisingly, the latter.

It was a long and tedious afternoon. Occasionally, to great excitement, a flight would be announced for boarding, and some of the crowd fought their way though the throng of others to get to one of the gates. There was still nowhere to sit, as by then even more people had arrived in the departure hall. Eventually I got an opportunity to claim a few square feet of floor to set down my case and sit on it. If I'd gone to ask a ground agent when, if ever, the flight would leave, I'd have lost my space. There would have been no point anyway – I couldn't see agents from any airline. Occasionally, one or two materialised when a flight boarded, but they disappeared immediately afterwards – it was safer for them to stay outside when they weren't busy, to avoid being attacked by frustrated passengers!

Through a sneaky look at baggage tags, I realised that the people sitting next to me were waiting for the same flight, so I said hello; they told me that they were regular passengers, and that no flight to Tacna was ever on time. At least it was reassuring to know that I hadn't inadvertently missed it and that I would not be left there on my own.

The flight did eventually leave at about 21:00; only eight hours late, with the board still showing 'on time'. Now, instead of arriving mid-afternoon, which I'd thought would allow me plenty of time to find a way of getting from Tacna airport to Arica, I was going to arrive very, very late. I had a hotel reservation in Arica, but was now reconciling myself to ending up spending the night in Tacna. I wondered what sort of place it was, and if I'd find any hotel there – I knew nothing about it, but was guessing that a small border town in Peru wasn't likely to have anything much.

Tacna's arrivals terminal didn't hold out any promise; it was rather like a small-town bus station (and it may well have doubled as that) at the end of a runway. Not that I spent any time looking around, it being 23:30. The plane had been packed, and there were hordes of people in the arrivals hall and the street outside, waiting to greet other passengers. I'd expected to be approached by taxi touts looking for business, making a beeline for me, as, very noticeably, the only non-Peruvian coming off the plane, but there were none. Outside on the street – not even asphalted – I couldn't see any taxis, but there were plenty of people to ask. I was pointed to a fairly ancient American car parked on the other side, with an equally ancient driver, who was fast asleep.

Once awoken, he was extremely enthusiastic about going to Arica, probably more so than me, and although haggling fares is normal, I hadn't the heart not to agree to the paltry $10 he asked for. "We have to drive very fast," he said, "to get there before the frontier closes." It had never occurred to me that the frontier would close, but it did, at midnight. 15km to go and 20 minutes left to get there and go through border formalities – assuming, that was, that the guards didn't knock off early. "And I cannot get a fare back in a Peruvian car", he added.

We careered at breakneck pace across the desert – although the only way to know it was desert was observing, in the weak glow of the headlights, the sand being blown up around us. The road didn't seem to be a road; no asphalt, no markings, nothing... but it was clear that the driver knew where it was, or where it was supposed to be, as he just drove on as fast as his poor old car would go, in a straight line over the perfectly flat terrain.

After ten minutes or so of total darkness, a few lights appeared far ahead of us, and five minutes later we reached them – the frontier post. 23:55. Five minutes to go, and it was still open.

Now, with the floodlighting, I could see around. It looked like a scene from a movie; the border post was a small hut; a couple of ancient military-looking jeeps stood parked, presumably for the guards; and all around in every direction, as far as the lights reached, flat sand, unbroken by vegetation, other buildings, cars, anything.

Not that there was time to stand about looking – the driver screeched to a halt, opened the doors, literally dragged me to the guard hut, and pushed a piece of paper into my hand. "Entry form! One minute before they close!"

Welcome to Chile.

The barrier came down behind us and the lights went out as we drove away (I'm guessing that anyone who arrives when the guard hut is closed could just drive round the barrier – I thought it a bit surreal and pointless having a barrier across a hypothetical road in the middle of a desert, but perhaps it looks more credible by day). Ten minutes later, we were in Arica. The driver had no problem finding my hotel – it was the only tall building in the city, with the name picked out in lights across the top.

Since he was obviously going to have to sleep the night in his car before he could recross the frontier, anything less than a $10 tip, doubling the fare, seemed mean; his enthusiastic acceptance proved it was more than enough to secure a guarantee of the services of 'the finest driver in Tacna' any time I felt like returning.

WEEK 2 - STOP 4
ARICA, CHILE

Arriving in Arica, the first thing anyone notices is the smell. Decaying fish. Not an appetising first impression.

A major local industry made pelleted fertiliser from dried fish, and the odour pervaded everywhere. Despite that, another important local business was tourism; Arica is a seaside town, and my hotel was obviously dedicated to holidaymakers. Looking out of my bedroom window in the morning, towards the Pacific Ocean, I could see vast expanses of beach beneath me – but also what was presumably the fertiliser factory dominating the southern end of town. I'm not a beach person, much less a fertiliser factory person, and the combination didn't look inviting. It made no sense to me why residents of the capital, Santiago, would make a three-hour flight north to holiday here when they have Valparaiso almost on their doorstep.

Apparently, they don't. The holidaymakers come from Bolivia. That's a landlocked country, and Arica is the nearest seaside town. They come despite the ubiquitous smell of dead fish, but not because they enjoy Chilean hospitality; Bolivians believe Arica is their birthright and consider it to be a city under enemy occupation. Back in the early nineteenth century, when the Spanish empire fell, Bolivians thought that Arica should have been ceded to them. Instead, it was claimed by Peru in a war of independence. Later, in the 1880s, the Pacific War saw it taken by Chile (they took Tacna as well, but returned that to Peru later). Locals told me that the Bolivians have never forgiven either Chile or Peru for not ceding Arica to them.

Arica means much more to Bolivia than a tourist destination. It's a free port, essential to its exports and imports. It's the terminus for a rail link to La Paz and an oil pipeline bringing crude from Bolivia to the coast for export.

Javier, my factory contact, came and picked me up from the hotel. Arica's not a big place, and the plant turned out to be so near that I could easily have walked to it. It didn't look like a factory; rather, it looked like a car dealership, with a single storey frontage with plate-glass windows. Inside, it looked more like a car repair workshop, but they did indeed build cars, or rather pickup trucks, assembling them from parts shipped in directly to the local port from Japan.

If I'd thought that the plant in Quito was a bit rough and ready, this one was a veritable cottage industry, if that's a term that can ever apply to assembling trucks. Not even a hint of a production line – more a case of "here's an empty space on the floor, let's build it here".

When planning the trip, I'd wondered why a big multinational would want to assemble vehicles in a place that appeared to be so far from anywhere, but, assuming it was economical on this scale, I could now see the logic; parts could be shipped in straight across the Pacific from Japan, there was a big demand for pickup trucks from the mining industry across the local desert area, and it was the only viable land route from the Pacific into Bolivia – the Andes cordillera presents very few crossing points.

The receptionist dusted off the visitors' book. Really. It's the only time in my life that the term 'dusted off' has been so literal. Desert dust, I supposed, that had had a good deal of time to settle, as I could see that I was the first visitor for over three years.

It took all of five minutes to inspect the electricity and water meters and confirm that they did indeed match up to the bills, and no time at all to arrange future ongoing liaison and an undying commitment on the part of Javier to use the system we were creating for them. So why go so far, for what seems so little? From a purely practical perspective, I got the accurate data we needed to deliver our contracted services to our client that we could never have got any other way. Far more importantly, though, what made the visit worthwhile was the recognition and welcome I got from everyone I met as the only 'head office' visitor that they'd had in a very long time. I consider myself a humble soul, but for them, it's like having a visit from royalty. When you're working for a huge multinational, but at a very small site in a very out-of-the-way location, knowing that you're remembered and are playing a key role is hugely important. And I'll never forget the huge smile of the head cook when I complimented her on her rice and beans.

Since I had plenty of time to spare, Javier asked me to give a presentation to the engineering team about energy management and the system we provided to the company. In the absence of a working laptop, this meant improvising with a flip chart, and, since it would have to be in Spanish, trying to remember all the technical terms. I recognise and understand the necessary vocabulary when I see the words written down, but never seem to be able to remember them in the heat of any pressured moment.

What they wanted was tips on new ways of saving energy, but it was such a small and simple factory, I couldn't think of a single thing they could do that they weren't already doing. There was no unusual equipment and no modern controls. They were already paranoid about switching off lights and turning off unnecessary equipment, though perhaps not as much as in Brazil. Given the antiquity of the wiring, I suspected that they were more interested in turning things off so as to not blow the fuses than because they wanted to use less and save energy and money.

Despite the length and hassle of the journey to get here and get away again, and whilst this could have been a crowning example of business trip futility, for me it was a happy day. I'd fulfilled the data collection mission. The team had seemed genuinely thrilled to be visited and get an impromptu presentation from a foreign 'expert'. I'd gone where few ventured, had an entertaining if nerve-wracking travel experience and, in the course of conversation over lunch, had even learnt a huge amount about the fertiliser and desert mining industries and the histories of Bolivia, Peru and Chile.

I actually felt quite sad to leave but needed to move on. My next and last factory visit would be in Rosario,

Argentina; there was no way of getting there direct from Arica, and I would have to route via Santiago.

Arica's airport was nothing like Tacna's; big, new and gleaming, and very busy, with plenty of flights, almost all of them to or from Santiago. Now I knew more about Arica, I guessed they relied on passengers who worked in the mining and fertiliser industries.

Chile's airline, LAN (since merged with Brazil's TAM to become LATAM), is long-established and efficient, and flies modern aircraft that feel safe. I knew the flight would be unremarkable – except for the view. Of all the flights in the world, the one where one absolutely must try to get a window seat – on the correct side of the aircraft – is the north-south flight over the long and narrow country of Chile. The views of the Andes are spectacular (though if you end up by the window on the other side, the Pacific coast view is marvellous too). In the late afternoon, with the setting sun shining directly onto the snow-capped peaks, it was sublime. The sort of flight that I'd happily stay on for hours. Occasionally I'd drag my eyes away from the window to look at my fellow passengers; all men, and all, I imagined, whether salespeople or miners, travelling for work of some kind; all either immersed in their laptops or books or asleep, none even remotely interested in the view. I suppose they'd seen it a lot more often than me. I'll never tire of it, and just writing this makes me want to be back there, viewing those majestic mountains from 39,000 feet.

WEEK 2 - STOP 5
ROSARIO, ARGENTINA

Santiago de Chile is a wonderful city, with a rich variety of interesting neighbourhoods. It's often remarked that Chile is the 'England of South America', and whilst I don't entirely agree, Santiago is perhaps the South American city least typical in terms of cultural style and architecture – it really does look and feel much more like a European capital. Maybe it's also because the people seem to be cooler, and less demonstrative. As in Buenos Aires and São Paulo, a high proportion of the people on the street look European, with relatively few *mestizos*. That's a relic of colonial times, when diseases introduced by conquistadores and missionaries wiped out most of the local population, followed by decades of European immigration. But that's just in the big cities. In Arica, for example, most of the population are American Indians – if you compared Arica with Santiago based only on the racial mix, you'd never guess that the cities were in the same country.

But this time, even though my connection was overnight, I wasn't going to venture into the city. Possessed by some sort of virtuous idiocy, I was determined to play the professional business traveller, single-mindedly fixated on the reasons for my trip, and committed to move on to my next destination as quickly as possible. Thus, I spent the night at the Holiday Inn at Santiago airport. Literally at the airport – one where it's not even necessary to leave the terminal, and you can walk straight from the plane to the room.

The business justification for anyone paying from their own or their company's pocket to stay in an on-airport hotel is that there's not enough time (or it would be a waste of time) to go into the city and back to the airport next morning, or that the inbound flight arrives too late, or the outbound leaves too early.

None of those applied to me for this trip.

I'd arrived early enough to make the city in time for dinner if I'd wanted to. My flight out wasn't until late morning, so I'd have had time for a leisurely breakfast and taxi ride back to the airport, maybe even a walk round the city first.

But, for whatever reason, I'd decided to stay in that Holiday Inn. These days, I might have read someone else's review on TripAdvisor before booking to stay there, and thought better of it. (One review is titled 'Most Depressing Night Ever'). I had an expansive view of a flat roof, with a tall and windowless and very dirty wall beyond them. The restaurant was bleaker still. I can still remember the burger!

What made it worse, sitting there, was thinking that I was missing out on a fine *Chanco a la Chilena* (pork) or another dish from the national cuisine that could have been mine had I gone into the city and, since I'd missed dinner in Arica, that my sole memory of Chilean cuisine from this trip was going to be this tasteless grey meat patty and greasy under-fried chips.

But by midday the next day I was once again sitting in a window seat, enjoying the view of the Andes, flying east this time, and savouring a glass of Chilean Merlot. Airlines served quite good quality wine in those days, even in Economy!

I'd anticipated a relaxing day; there was only one daily flight from Santiago to Rosario. As that was in the middle of the day, there was no time for any seriously productive work either before or after. For once on this trip, I'd given myself time in the afternoon to explore. I'd expected the city to be small, but no; looking out, as the plane circled to land, it seemed enormous. Well over a million live there and because most houses are single storey, like Sorocaba in Brazil and many other South American cities, it straggles on for miles in every direction from the centre. Cities like this can cover the same land area as some European or North American cities that have five times the population.

So, time to get excited! A new city! Not my first time in Argentina, though; I'd been before, on a long touring holiday, and fallen in love with it then. I'm often asked what my favourite country is, and my standard reply is that I like all of them – I just love travelling. In truth, though, when pressed, I have to admit that my heart goes back to Argentina as much as, or more than, any other country I've visited.

Perhaps it's the enormous variety of scenery and different climates; desert fringed by the Andes in the

North, the rugged Peninsula Valdes in the East with its wild coast, populated by seals and penguins, the lake district around Bariloche that's redolent of Switzerland, the Perito Moreno glacier in the South, and, further south still, the cold and windswept port of Ushuaia, the point of departure for Antarctic cruises and supply vessels. Perhaps it's the wonderful city of Buenos Aires, where wide avenues fringed with the Italianate architecture of government buildings in the centre gives way to brightly coloured repurposed warehouses along the waterfront, a city honed by a Latin culture that's highlighted by turning a corner and chancing on a tango class, performing in the middle of the street. Perhaps it's the food and drink, especially meat. A country for carnivores. Across all of South America, fine beef is cultivated and served with care and passion; in Argentina, though, beef becomes a religion. If you like steak, you'll find none finer than here. Accompanied, naturally, by my favourite wine – Malbec – fermented from grapes grown high on the Andes foothills in estates surrounding the city of Mendoza.

It's all of those things taken singly and together. No doubt if I lived there I'd like it less; for every country I've spent considerable time in – USA, Spain, Brazil, India, China, my home country of the UK – my initial enthusiasm has, over the years, been tempered into a sort of love-hate relationship, perhaps comparable to getting married but before long contemplating the divorce.

In all those other countries, the thing I've come to love most is the people. That's not true of Argentina.

I may have been unlucky, and of course people aren't all the same in any country, but one can always find some national traits, a fashion of living, a style of talking, an inclusivity. At least as seen from the viewpoint of a foreigner; natives will usually deny that there's any uniformity. In my opinion, Argentinians are not naturally friendly, or at least not to foreigners; they have a rather aggressive-sounding variant of Spanish, difficult for foreigners to understand and, particularly in business meetings, most people that I've met act in a rather superior manner. Given the country's history and continuing propensity to economic disaster, such an attitude seems misplaced. It's possibly just my own experience; but many others I've talked to agree.

It's nothing to do with my being British. When I first went in the 90s, and even at the time of this visit in 2002, memories of the war over the Malvinas (Falkland Islands) were still strong. Back on that first trip, I'd been advised to tell people, if asked, that I was Irish – I'd followed the principle, but said I was Australian instead. Plenty of English people used to think my accent sounded vaguely antipodean, and as I definitely can't do an Irish accent, I thought I'd be on safer ground. Over time, I found it didn't make any difference; the attitude to foreigners was the same, wherever one came from, and in none of my visits have I met anyone who demonstrated negativity specifically towards Brits.

Except, perhaps, the immigration officer at Rosario airport. More likely he just hadn't seen a British passport before, and that he had plenty of time; it was the only international flight that day and, as Chileans can just stroll in, there was once again only one passenger – me – in the line for 'Other Foreigners'. So, turn a page in the passport, examine each of the stamps, turn back to the photo page, look forensically at me, look back at the passport, turn another page, look at the stamps there, go back to the photo page... lots of stamps in my passport, lots of pages to look at. You get the picture. After my experience in Quito, I was preparing my speech in case he tried telling me I needed a business visa. It must have been at least 10 minutes before he decided that he couldn't think of a reason to arrest me, or delay me further, found a new page that met his liking, and added a new stamp. Welcome to Argentina.

The factory I'd be visiting the next day was quite a way out of town, but I'd chosen to stay in the so-called historic centre. First impressions didn't suggest it was very historic, but the buildings were clearly older and the streets narrower than the suburban ones I'd been driven through, coming from the airport in a *remise* (taxi).

Since it was getting late in the afternoon, my first priority after checking in had to be shopping – for shoes. Argentina was, and remains, an incredibly cheap country for products they make or grow, and that includes shoes. I suppose the leather comes cheap, being a by-product of all the cattle; the manufacturing quality is outstanding, and, as I'd discovered on my first visit, the price is better still; a pair of shoes, almost identical to ones that then cost £100 in London, cost only about £20 in Argentina.

Easy to find styles I liked; difficult to get them in the right size. It seems no Argentine shoe shop ever stocks any style in more than just one random size. I suspect that they won't invest in stock they might not sell, but whatever the reason, it makes for a frustrating trail round lots of shoe shops before finding one that I like and that fits.

Mission accomplished, I set off to explore. Leaving the shops behind, I found narrower streets with older buildings.

The streets here were so empty, I thought I'd left mankind behind too, until I turned a corner and found a long queue of mostly young people lining the pavement. The queue went around the block, ending at the door of the Spanish Consulate. I was curious as to why they were all waiting. The girl at the front told me that she'd been there since 5am – over twelve hours. Apparently at some time 'soon', someone would open the doors, and she, and an unknown but limited number of others behind her, would be able to claim a ticket that would gain her entry to the embassy in Buenos Aires on another future day to apply for Spanish citizenship.

Spain (and Italy and Portugal too, I believe) had a scheme whereby those with grandparents who had been their citizens, whether or not they were still alive, and had paperwork to prove it, could claim nationality. The young people were queueing because there was a rumour that the scheme was going to end soon. However, I think it's still in existence. Argentina is a wonderful country; but, despite the fine words and efforts of successive governments of different political persuasions, its economy always seems to be in an abysmal state; for young people in search of a better future, a European passport offers incalculable value. Well worth queuing all day for. And probably tomorrow too – the girl at the front of the line said she didn't think they'd give out many tickets, so most of those waiting behind her would go home disappointed.

Winding my way onwards, down towards the Parana river, there were more and more people, masses of them, coming out of buildings, pouring out of side streets, all headed in the same direction. Locals, not tourists, and certainly not business visitors like me with a little time on their hands and out for an exploratory stroll. Their destination was a big square, the Plaza de 25 de Mayo.

In every city in every country of South America, there are squares, avenues, streets and parks with names that commemorate dates. There's always one for the date of independence from Spain (or in the case of Brazil, from Portugal). In Argentina, there are two dates in contention – 25th May 1810, the date of the first revolution, which this square in Rosario commemorates, and 9th July, the date of the formal Declaration of Independence in 1816. Unsurprisingly, there is a road named after that too – and a sports centre, a school, and even a car park and an internet café.

But back to the Plaza. As the crowd swept me towards it, past the cathedral, a brass band struck up. No ordinary band. There, in the centre of the square, in front of a very large cenotaph topped by the national flag, hundreds of soldiers were massed. The brass band was all dressed in camouflage type uniform, so unremarkable. Beyond them, though, stood a far greater number of men, all dressed like human versions of classic tin soldiers; dark blue jackets, white shirts, red sashes and black top hats. Definitely not 21st century military uniform; I'd have thought that they were actors had they not, on a drum roll, unshouldered their rifles and fired into the air.

Someone jammed next to me in the crowd told me that the Monument to the Flag is one of the most important sites in Argentina; it was where General Manuel Belgrano raised the new Argentine flag for the first time in 1812. The flag was raised again in this ceremony. I still don't know what exactly was being commemorated; it didn't seem to be the anniversary of anything, and although I asked the man next to me, I didn't understand his explanation. Anyway, I was left in no doubt that it was a big event for local and national pride. Given that, and the relevance to the ceremony and location of General Belgrano (the navy boat famously sunk by the British in the Falklands/Malvinas War was named after him), I decided this was one time to tell my neighbour and informant, when he asked where I was from, that I was Australian!

Indeed, if I visited Rosario again, even after all these years, I might well do the same. Just a few years after that visit, just on the opposite side of the Avenida Belgrano that runs past the monument, parallel to the river, they have constructed a huge new 'Monument to the Fallen in Malvinas' and renamed the park in which it stands the 'National Park of Allegiance'. Personally, I have no interest in whether those remote islands stay as British Falklands or revert to being Argentine Malvinas. They're in the middle of the Atlantic and I don't really understand how either country can lay claim to them, so I'd be content either way; but it's probably safe to assume that the locals might expect a Briton to be prejudiced.

Ceremony over, I wandered the short distance down to the Parana river, over the ground where that park now stands; back then, there was nothing to see except grassy banks lined with men holding or guarding long fishing rods, hundreds of them, spaced two or three metres apart from each other, stretching as far as the eye could see. The Parana is a big river – in South America, second only to the Amazon – and wide and deep enough to be navigable by big ships for hundreds of miles from Buenos Aires, past

Rosario and north to Paraguay. And presumably full of fish, though I didn't see anyone catching any.

Now it was getting dark, and I was hungry. And there, right on cue, was the Club Nautico. I wasn't a member, and I didn't have a yacht, but neither of those proved a barrier to entry. A flunky, uniformed almost as impressively as the tin soldiers I'd watched in the ceremony, welcomed me into a beautiful, huge restaurant and gave me a big table, all to myself, overlooking the river. No sunset – it's the wrong side of the river, looking east – but with soothing views of big barges, each now lit up in the fading light as they slowly passed up or down river. More soothing still, a large glass of Malbec, and a far too large (well, perhaps not) and extremely rare *Bife de Chorizo*, my favoured Argentine steak (it's the same cut as New York Strip, and close to sirloin). Ah, I thought, it can be a tough life, this business travelling!

The next morning, though, I had to get back to business. The car plant I was visiting was about half an hour south of Rosario, surrounded by open country. Beyond the city boundary, green fields just went on and on, until the plant's water tower – a feature of almost all car factories worldwide – appeared on the horizon. Getting closer, it looked like a standard modern plant; a huge, low, square, grey shed, surrounded by a barbed wire fence. My *remise* dropped me at the first gate he found, insisting it was the correct and indeed the only one. As he sped off and I walked towards the guard hut, I hoped he was right – if there was another gate, I couldn't see it, and it would be a very long walk around the perimeter to get there.

Fortunately, the taxi driver was correct. Even though it looked deserted, it was the right gate. Just no other visitors, neither coming nor going. The certainty of no interruptions gave the security guard an opportunity to shine and prove that he should really have been a bureaucrat, starting with making me complete a long form with what seemed to be my entire life history and sign several pages of terms and conditions, mostly of a health and safety nature, that appeared to make me solely liable not only for my own safety but anything whatsoever that might happen to anyone anywhere within the confines of the plant while I was on the premises. I'd never had quite so much paperwork to complete in order to get into a factory before.

Satisfied with that, he then laboriously removed the batteries to read and log the serial numbers of my two cell phones – the Blackberry that didn't work in Argentina, and the Nextel brick phone that I had bought just for a couple of countries – Argentina and Brazil – and couldn't make to work either. I'd happily have left both phones and the rest of my luggage at the gatehouse, but the guard told me that wasn't allowed. I suppose because it would have done him out of sticking labels on them. These procedures were all taking a long time. I must have been standing there for half an hour already.

Someone entered the guard hut from the plant side and tried talking to the guard.

"*Momento*! I'm busy with this man, you will have to wait!"

Returning to his officialdom, that he was clearly greatly enjoying, the guard took down a box from a shelf, removed a sheet of sticky labels with holograms, wrote the number of one of the labels on one of the forms I'd filled in, peeled it off, and stuck it onto the Blackberry.

Then he started on the 'brick', turning it over and over, looking at it from every angle; I asked him why.

"I have to cover up the camera lens with one of these labels."

"It doesn't have a camera."

"I think it does – on this model it is hidden!"

"I don't think so."

"Oh yes it does. They all do! I cannot let you take a camera onto the site."

"Why don't I just leave the phone here and collect it when I leave?"

"You might need it."

"No. It doesn't work."

I didn't have the heart to tell him that my Blackberry was an old model that didn't have a camera either, and he'd stuck the label over the on/off button. I was beginning to fear that if I made any more comments, I'd be getting a full body strip-search.

Paperwork complete, checked and filed, and finally, apparently satisfied that he had thwarted my spying intentions, he picked up the phone and dialled. He listened for a while. "Your contact is not answering. You will have to wait."

"That's because my contact is already here, standing next to the phone on the other side of your desk." I could read his badge at that distance.

So, finally, I made it in.

You might think that visiting a factory where you've been invited, are expected, and come with the authority of 'Head Office', should be straightforward enough. You might also think that a major global company with around 100 plants around the world would have the same front desk security arrangements everywhere. You'd be wrong on both counts.

The fundamental rules are the same. However, as I'd discovered on this trip, local interpretation varies not only by country but by individual plant, and quite possibly by individual security guard. Plants that get lots of visitors every day, and regular visits from HQ, like the ones in Brazil, might have a lot of red tape, but the guards are generally very efficient and pleasant about it. Those that hardly ever get any visitors, like Arica, tend to forget that there are any rules at all, other than perhaps the token gesture of getting a signature in the visitors' book. Then there are those like Rosario, somewhere in-between the two extremes, where a security guard with little to do will dot every 'i' and cross every 't', and invent a few more squiggles along the way. Those ones are irritating or worse, but I don't blame them; the one who processed me at Rosario could very well have been thinking that, especially since I was a foreigner from 'Head Office', if he skipped or skimped any procedures he might get a high level dressing-down at best, the sack at worst. He wasn't to know that I was only there for the mundane exercise of finding electricity and water meters and matching them up with the bills.

José Manuel, who'd been patiently waiting on the other side of the desk, didn't seem to be too clear about why I was there either. He took me first to meet his boss, the Head of Engineering. His greetings were very polite, though, until I refused a cup of *yerba mate*, Argentina's answer to tea. Most people there drink it all day, from their personal special cup and through a metal straw, but it's one drink I strongly dislike. I lost a lot of brownie points by turning up my nose at *mate*.

After half an hour of cross-examination in thick Argentine Spanish, which I struggled to understand and had to keep asking him to repeat, I worked out that the boss and his subordinate believed me to be an expert on waste water treatment. They wouldn't accept my saying that I wasn't, I think they just thought I was being modest.

Rather later, I concluded that the reason why they thought I knew all about water treatment was that it happened to be the specialist subject of the Head Office manager who had first written to them to introduce me. But not before they had walked me to the furthest corners of the site ('furthest' being no exaggeration) to admire and comment on their water treatment plants. To my untutored eye, they looked good – insofar as a concrete room, filled with a tangle of pipes and pumps, can look good – and they were demonstrably proud of them. Even to the extent that they harangued a poor technician who we met in one of them for not having adequately polished a big stopcock. Not being able to think of anything I could say that would be constructive, I resorted to congratulating them on excellently designed and maintained equipment – I just hoped that it really was!

I should perhaps explain that water treatment is a Big Thing in car plants. Lots and lots of water is used in the process of treating and painting vehicles, and the effluent is poisonous. Municipal sewerage treatment plants can't deal with toxic chemicals, so the waste water can't be discharged to sewers as it is, especially in places where they might, in turn, discharge into rivers or the sea. The factory water treatment plants remove the nasty stuff and, even if the result isn't water you'd want to drink or bathe in, at least it wouldn't kill you, or the fish in the rivers or lakes it might end up in.

Water is also expensive, and in some places in short supply, so industrial water recycling has been a worthy ambition for many years – much longer than the drums of ecological concern have been beating.

I managed to steer the subject back to verifying electricity (and water) bills and locating the meters for long enough to get the information I needed. And just in time for lunch, where, having queued in the canteen and piled my plate with rice and beans and a few other things, my companion piloted me to a table headed by the Engineering Manager, accompanied by what must have been his whole team, where I was invited to share my opinions on water treatment with everyone.

I guess I passed the test, whatever that test might have been, as everyone was nodding happily, and nobody asked any tough questions, but it went on much longer than a normal canteen lunch would, and I was glad that I had an excuse to get away. I'd asked my *remise* driver to pick me up at the same gate at 2.30pm. José Manuel got me there exactly on time. I bid my farewell, signed out in the visitors' book, on doing which, and with a theatrical flourish, the security guard removed the sticker over the on/off button on my non-functional Blackberry.

However, there was no car and driver waiting. I supposed he'd turn up soon. I sat on the bench outside the guard's hut to wait. At first, I felt pretty relaxed; I had lots of time, my flight wasn't until 6pm. But, as time passed, my mood changed. It wasn't just nerves or impatience, though both were growing. It was just a depressing place to hang around. In front of me, a view over miles of open green fields, the motorway out of sight, just a single road snaking up to the gate. Too boring to be idyllic. No traffic, no movement of any kind. Behind me, a tall chain-link fence topped with razor wire. Altogether, a bit creepy.

Thirty minutes felt more like a few hours. I was used to things not running on time, especially in South America but, even there, taxi drivers are usually pretty reliable for pre-booked trips, and this one already knew from the morning run that I was a fairly generous tipper. Unwisely, I'd failed to ask him for a phone number – but anyway, in those days, it would have been unlikely that he'd have had a mobile. Time to give up waiting.

Back to the hut to ask the guard to call me a *remise*. No, he couldn't make outside calls from his phone, or at least that's what he said (hopefully there was an exception for the emergency services). He could call José Manuel, who in turn could call for a car. Fifteen long minutes later, JoséManuel came back to see me. He told me that he'd tried calling a few taxis, but none of them could come out. He didn't know why. He was going to ask his boss if he could take me to the airport himself. The security guard allowed me to go back into the plant with him, this time without any new bureaucracy or sticky labels.

That was kind of him, but it wasn't a matter of just jumping in his car and heading off to the airport. First, he had to get permission to leave the site during working hours. That wasn't as simple as just asking his boss; rather, the bureaucracy required him first to go to HR – in another building – to get a form (in triplicate of course), then fill in the form, get it signed by his manager, take it back to HR, and get someone there to sign it. They kept one copy and gave him back the other two.

He told me that he wasn't allowed to take me in his own car. Maybe he just didn't want to. Maybe he didn't even have one. I didn't know, and I never found out. But borrowing a company car was a major exercise. Heavens, the factory actually built the cars – over a thousand of them every day – so you'd think that it ought to be easy, but no.

Time was marching on, and so were we. First to the transport office, where, after waiting for the man behind the desk to finish what seemed like an interminable phone call, José Manuel handed in his form and, in exchange, got another one he needed to complete, this time in quadruplicate. Then back to his boss to get his signature on it. By the time we got through all the bureaucracy, found the car, made it to the gate, had all the paperwork checked again and had been allowed past the barrier, it had taken more than an hour. By now it was well after 4pm.

We'd also had to leave by a different gate (which only went to prove my morning driver wrong when he had told me that there was only one), so we then had to drive round the perimeter to the first one just in order to sign me out again and for me to give back my badge.

Finally, we were on the road to the airport. At least it was a wide dual carriageway, with very little traffic; the airport is on the opposite side of the city to the factory, but it's not that far, and I figured we'd be there in about half an hour. Plenty of time, then. I forgot the tension of the previous hour or two and relaxed.

At least, I did until we crested a hill and saw, perhaps a kilometre ahead of us, a barrage of flashing lights and a large crowd of people standing in the road. As we slowed and approached, the view became clearer; it was a demonstration, with several hundred people brandishing placards and a dozen or so police cars with their flashing beacons on, blocking the road to prevent progress in either direction.

"They work for the city – they have not paid them for a few months, so they're demonstrating," José Manuel explained.

They didn't look like they'd be going anytime soon – and there was no way through. I got the sinking feeling that my attempts to get away from Rosario that day had finally been completely frustrated.

José Manuel, however, wasn't giving up so easily. He didn't want to be stuck there any more than I did. We were slowing down, still a few hundred metres from the line of stationary traffic ahead of us, when he spotted a gap in the central reservation. Not a proper access, mind, just somewhere where the crash barrier had been removed. Screeching to a halt, he simply turned, drove across through the gap onto the other carriageway, and accelerated away, back in the direction we'd just come from, leaving the demonstrators and police behind us.

"Isn't that illegal?" I said.

"Obviously – but the police are busy down there, and anyway, now other cars have followed us." Looking behind me, I could see he was right.

"We'll leave at the next exit and simply drive across the city. It'll take a bit longer, but we'll get there."

137

It was actually a lot longer. Either we'd hit the rush hour, or everyone else was avoiding the motorway, or both, but the traffic was just crawling along. By the time we finally approached the airport, I'd already reconciled myself to missing the plane and having to stay over in Rosario. It wouldn't have been a big issue for me; my reason for going to Buenos Aires was there were no flights back to London from Rosario. I wasn't flying home for a couple of days; it was an opportunity to relax first in one of my favourite cities. But José Manuel was determined we'd get to the airport as soon as possible; hopefully the plane would be late.

We pulled up to the terminal at 5.45pm – just 15 minutes before my scheduled departure. The road outside was totally quiet; just one taxi sitting there, no people at all around. Perhaps everyone else was stuck on the highway. Inside, it was as eery as only an empty airport terminal can be. Not completely empty though; there was a girl standing behind one of the check-in desks, the one for my flight. She didn't look much like a check-in agent, dressed in casual clothes, but she waved as I walked in – obviously I was expected.

My reservation was with AeroTaxi, which was a very small domestic airline. I think they mostly operated as on-demand air taxis, living up to their name, but they had two or three "normal" scheduled services, including the one I wanted, from Rosario to Buenos Aires. Whilst I had confirmed my reservation by phone, I didn't have a ticket.

There was no need, though. I handed the fare to the girl, in cash, and in return she gave me a plain white card on which someone had written, in felt-tip pen, 'Boarding Pass' on one side, and the number '9' on the other. Just like TAME, but tackier. To my greater surprise, she told me to climb over the scales to her side of the desk, where she opened the door behind her. It led straight onto the tarmac. She pointed at a tiny propeller plane parked about a hundred metres away. "Go, quickly!"

No, no security. Not even a security guard. Nobody in sight except a man in uniform standing by the plane, who turned out to be the pilot. There were other passengers, though – eight of them, all already on the plane. I was number 9. The pilot took my boarding pass, ticked me off a list he had on a clipboard, and grabbed my bag from me.

It was a very small plane for a commercial flight, the first time I'd ever flown on anything so tiny. It only took nine passengers, in three rows – one window seat on each side of each row, and a fold-down seat in the middle. The plane had two propeller engines, one on each wing, and a very dodgy-looking baggage compartment right at the back of the fuselage close to the tail. The pilot opened the door to it, which was basically just secured by a twist catch, forced my bag inside since the compartment was already full, and closed the latch again. I remember waving goodbye to it, thinking that the latch was bound to come undone somewhere in flight, and my bag and all the others would drop out, landing in some remote bit of country between Rosario and Buenos Aires, or possibly in the Parana river.

I climbed aboard into the last seat. I had what I supposed was the advantage of sitting by the door that doubled as the emergency exit, and the disadvantage of being horribly cramped and uncomfortable, as the handle stuck into my elbow on the left, and the man on the right was rather large. Never mind; it was only an hour's flight, and I'd made it on board.

So, much to my amazement, considering the afternoon I'd had, the little plane, with me on it, took off exactly on schedule at 6pm. Now expecting what was left of the day to be uneventful, I started thinking about dinner...

But this wasn't a plane for napping or daydreaming. If it wasn't noisy enough already, as soon as he levelled off, the pilot turned in his seat and started shouting at us. The combination of the engine noise, his thick Argentine accent and my bad Spanish meant I had little clue what exactly he was saying, but I understood enough to realise it was nothing terrible, just the safety briefing. Well, I flew so often I knew that off by heart, for jet aircraft at least. I had my seatbelt on. I definitely knew where the emergency exit was – the handle was jabbing into my upper arm. I heard nothing about lifejackets, but figured that even if there were any, apart from not being able to reach it if it was under my seat, it would be unlikely to be of any use in an emergency on this little aircraft, even if the route did track the Rio Parana.

Given the small and cramped aircraft and short route, all I was hoping for was the quickest and safest flight possible. The last thing I was expecting was any inflight service. However, about ten minutes into the flight, the pilot reached beneath his legs and, rather like a magician finding rabbits in hats, started pulling out cartons of juice and packets of biscuits and tossing them back over his shoulder. As I was right behind him, I was responsible for passing them on to other passengers. That's the nearest I've ever got to being a cabin service attendant.

A very loud crash shattered that happy dream of an alternative career. It sounded like something hitting the side of the aircraft, and the plane instantly went into a dive, rocking wildly from side to side. Grown men around me screamed. I suppose I did too; I know that right then I was more scared than on any other flight I've ever taken, even the TAME one from Bogotá to Quito the week before.

But the pilot managed to level off the plane again and turned his head to look behind him. He pointed at the window on the opposite side to where I was sitting. This was when I discovered, for a fact, reassuringly, that aircraft windows are double-glazed. The outer pane of that window was completely shattered.

It wasn't because we'd been hit by lightning. After we landed at Aeroparque in Buenos Aires, a nerve-wracking thirty minutes later, and disembarked, the pilot showed us what had happened – the tip of one of the blades on the propeller on that side had come off, and presumably hit the side of the plane, shattering the window and denting the fuselage. For me, another close shave. The pilot behaved as if it was just another day at his office.

The propeller tip turned missile hadn't hit the baggage compartment, and my fears of the catch coming undone mid-air had proven unfounded. Nevertheless, my poor wheely case had suffered. In fact, it came out of the flight in a worse state than I did. In the course of being forced in amongst all the other cases, or being pulled out, the frame had got twisted, and it didn't wheel any more. Never mind. That would be easy and cheap to replace, and give me an excuse for doing a bit of shopping in Buenos Aires. Lifting it by the handle, which hadn't come off, I went in the direction of the taxi rank for the short ride into the city.

Like so many South American airlines, AeroTaxi didn't last long; by the time of my next visit to Argentina, a year or so later, and being brave enough to want to risk flying with them again, I discovered that it had gone bust. I was told that they'd had a fatal crash, not long after my flight from Rosario. A sobering tale that reminded me of my own experience and made sure I'd never forget it.

CONCLUSION

12 days, 7 countries, 8 flights, 12,939 miles flown (so far, and another 7000 to get back to London), 10 different hotels – was it all worth it?

Of course it was.

Although all I had to show for my labours in tangible physical form was a case full of scruffy, scrawled-on, oil-stained energy bills, and a bookful of notes, I'd achieved my aim. I'd got all the information needed to get the nine South American factories onto the system, established good and lasting relationships with local engineers and managers that would help ensure future success and, I believe, contributed substantially to retaining and growing one of my company's biggest clients.

And I'd had a ball doing it!

What we learnt in handling, processing and analysing the data we subsequently received from all these sites that I had visited in South America enabled us to both adapt our systems to handle them as efficiently as the data from the UK and North America, and to manage day-to-day liaison with overseas operations with different languages and in different time zones. Our US business grew, and we could go after big companies that also had operations across Latin America; unlike the car manufacturer, that had a few sites using a lot of energy, we now had international banks that had hundreds of sites all using only modest amounts of energy.

But now we had a different challenge. These new clients also had sites in China, Japan, Korea... The data coming from those countries was not only different, but was written in languages we couldn't decipher.

Time to make another long business trip...

PART TWO

A FAR EASTERN BUSINESS ODYSSEY

Southeast Asia

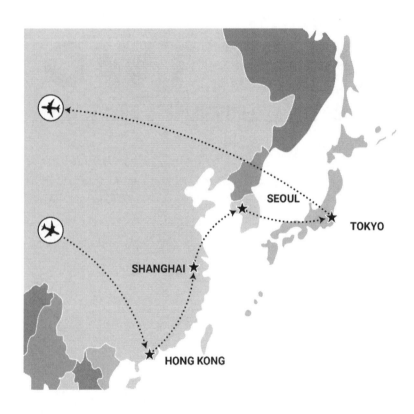

SEOUL

TOKYO

SHANGHAI

HONG KONG

INTRODUCTION

It's April 2006. It's a Saturday. I'm walking through a market in Seoul, Korea, having a very public screaming match with a young Chinese-Korean woman whom I have recently promoted to Asia-Pacific Regional Manager. Despite the promotion, she is not happy. I think she wants my job. Right now, I'd happily give it to her if it would shut her up and calm me down. If I'd wanted a screaming match, I could have stayed at home; no, correct that, I've never had a domestic dispute as loud and unpleasant as this is turning out to be.

Why am I arguing with her and getting more and more upset? Go on any longer, and murderous thoughts might surface. I turn on my heel and walk away. Will she follow me or go off on her own? Do I care? I assume she'll make her way back to the hotel, and that I'll see her tomorrow morning at breakfast, acting as if nothing ever happened. That seems to be the way it goes. Certainly, that's how it's gone for the last fortnight; but there's still one more week of this business trip left. The conflict makes me feel like packing it in. I've felt like that on other days, but then there's been a new meeting with a big and possibly valuable new customer, and it all feels worthwhile again. Despite the fighting.

Why am I here, anyway?

To explain, I need to go back about three months earlier, to the first week of January, to be precise.

Back then, in 2006, it seemed like every big business – and certainly many of our company's biggest customers – were focused on expanding in China and other countries in the Far East. To deliver the services we'd promised them, the same ones as we had been delivering for years in Britain and America, we needed to process and analyse data from those countries. By the end of the previous year, we'd realised that this was becoming a big problem for us. We didn't have any staff who could read and write and speak the Asian 'sign languages', and even if we hired them, which I supposed ought to be easy enough in London, we would still face the struggle of the time difference of seven or eight hours when we needed to call them, or if they wanted to talk to us. The nearest office we had was in India, but there it was more or less impossible to hire staff fluent in Chinese, Japanese, Korean or the other Asian languages, and there was still a big time difference.

So, we ended 2005 with an ever-growing pile of paper documents we found incomprehensible, and therefore couldn't process, and an ever-growing backlog of calls we needed to make.

I'd hoped that my December holiday would clear my

mind and bring inspiration, but I found myself back at my desk on 2nd January with no solution and with this still our biggest headache.

We did have one Chinese employee in London – a young lady called Jin-Ae. She hadn't been employed because she was Chinese, and she was working on a completely different project, not related to China or the Far East at all. She was well-qualified too, and obviously didn't want a routine job; we couldn't ask her to start to input data from bills. Jin-Ae hadn't been with us for long, but she'd proved herself to be highly competent and a hard worker. The only negative was that she was not popular with colleagues. I did not know why. Perhaps I should have asked around. But she'd seemed fine to me, not that I'd ever spent more than a few minutes in her company. When I had, I'd noticed she was quite outspoken. She never hesitated to give her opinion, unasked for. A trait that I liked; others obviously didn't. I decided to ask her opinion on our Asian data problem. Maybe she'd have some ideas.

"Do you know anyone who would like a part-time job processing Chinese data for us? Or can you help me find an outsourcing company who can do the work for us?"

"At last you ask me. Why have you not asked me before? I have a plan already."

I suppose it should have been obvious to me to ask her before, but I hadn't, and I felt a bit stupid now. But I didn't want to show that.

"Excellent! Tell me."

"We set up a new operation in China, just like the one in India."

"We only have enough work for one input clerk and one customer support person – that's not enough to justify a new operation."

"Simple. We just get more customers from China and Japan and Korea. We go and sell to the big international companies there, like Sony and Samsung. Then we will have a lot of work."

"We can't sell to them. We don't speak Japanese or Korean."

"But I do. I will sell. You will see."

Ah, if it were only so simple… getting new work and selling new projects is never easy. It's hard enough getting a meeting with a decision-maker in a major company in one's own country. But it's always good to find someone who's so totally confident. And, to my mind, there's no employee more welcome or appreciated by a business owner than one who not only comes up with a practical solution but is prepared to put in the effort to turn it into reality.

I'd also not known that Jin-Ae could speak and write all three languages fluently – or at least, that's what she claimed.

And thus, a plan was hatched. Jin-Ae would be relieved of her current project and dedicate herself for the next three months to establishing useful Far East contacts and, specifically, to plan a three-week business trip to China, Japan and Korea, one week in each country. China, to find either an outsourcing company or, better still, a potential partner with whom we could build a Chinese joint venture operation to process data and handle customer support. Japan and Korea, to try to sell our services to their big multinational companies, with the objective of increasing our Far East business volume to a level that would sustain the planned Chinese operation.

On condition that she could put together an itinerary with a worthwhile programme of confirmed meetings with potential partners or customers that would keep us usefully busy every working day, I agreed that I would go with her on the entire trip. For me, this was an unusual and enormous commitment, as I was always busy, and three weeks was a long trip by my standards. I had to trust that she would succeed; it was a gamble, but I had no alternatives.

THREE MONTHS IN THE PLANNING

Jin-Ae took to the project with alacrity. However early I got in to the office in the morning – and I was often there by 7.30am, even earlier when we had a crisis – she would already be at her desk, jabbering away loudly in her high-pitched voice in Mandarin or Japanese or Korean; I couldn't tell between them. With the time difference, it was the only way she could reach people when they were in their offices. Crack of dawn for us, nearly going-home time for them.

Every so often she'd come to my desk to tell me of a new triumph, having made some valuable contact or arranged an important meeting. From what I could see, the planning seemed to be going really well. In early March, she asked me for an hour's meeting.

She started by asking me to check my diary for specific dates when we would travel; could we spend four weeks instead of three, as we would have a lot of meetings, and she could organise even more? No, I said, let's stick to a three-week schedule; I don't mind how many meetings we have each day. Let's try to do as much as possible in the time we have allowed.

Almost all my business travel was solo. Even though I crave company when I'm on my own, I rarely travelled with others. When I had gone in company, it had always been with colleagues I'd known for a long time and got on with well, but even then, two or three days was about the limit for me (and possibly too much for them!). A three-week trip to the other side of the planet with a relative stranger was quite something. But, even if I'd wanted to, this wasn't a trip I could do on my own. As she pointed out, I would need a translator in all the meetings, so she could fulfil that function, and if I wanted her to contribute too, as she correctly assumed I would, she'd need an important title on her business cards, since we could safely assume that almost everyone we were likely to meet would be male and misogynistic. Arm twisted effectively, I agreed she could assume the title of Far East Regional Manager, and use it straight away, but told her that any appropriate salary increase would only happen after a successful trip.

We agreed on dates, staying, as we'd first discussed, one week in each of the three countries. Until I'd put the dates in my diary and booked my first flight, she refused to believe I was committed, and she would not leave the meeting room. To fit in with my schedule and her personal commitments, we agreed we would fly in and out of Asia separately, starting in Hong Kong and finishing in Tokyo, but between those two points, we'd travel together and stay in the same hotels.

Finally satisfied that I was as serious as she was, she went away to finalise the itinerary. It was impressive; we had meetings every day over the three weeks so, since we'd also need time to prepare and refine presentations, make notes, take follow-up actions and, at least in my case, get on with the day job by email and phone with our operations in the UK, USA and India, there wouldn't be any spare time when we'd be idle, except at weekends, when there could be opportunity to do a little sightseeing.

Our last planning meeting was in London, about a week before we were due to leave. For the first time, I saw her looking really nervous. I'd never known her to be in any mood other than over-confident, so I was surprised.

"What's wrong?"

"I am embarrassed."

"What do you mean?"

"I am worried you will not make a good impression."

"Why do you think that?"

She told me that she had three over-riding concerns – and they were all about me.

First, she was worried that I might have booked very downmarket hotels, to save money. Since we would have some of our contacts meeting us at hotels or picking us up from them, she was afraid it would make our business look cheap and nasty. I couldn't fathom why; she had the list of hotels I'd booked, and they were all rated four or five stars. It took a while for me to realise that she had just never heard of the names of chains like Marriott and InterContinental. I was amused. Hearing what came next, though, I should probably have started to get worried.

"Why did you think that I'd book bad hotels?"

"Because you do not act like a boss here. You sit in open plan. You don't have a boss's desk. You don't have a boss's car."

Well, true; it wasn't a Merc or BMW or Jag – it was a Saab. New, but a Saab nonetheless. Since I didn't as a rule drive customers or prospects about, or show off or talk about what car I owned, it had never occurred to me that anyone would think that what I drove implied meanness or inferiority, or whatever she was interpreting it to be.

I did my best to reassure her that I wouldn't be telling anyone in China that I drove a Saab, let alone show anyone a picture of it, and that all the hotels were good. She seemed pacified, but I figured she wouldn't give me the benefit of the doubt until she'd actually checked into one.

Her next worry was that we needed business cards. Hundreds, perhaps a thousand of them. Double-sided, English on one side and Chinese, Korean or Japanese on the other, so three sets. It's true that both business cards and job titles are very important in the Far East; one is handing out and receiving cards all the time (with both hands) and the job titles, as stated on them, are studied closely. She wasn't worried I wouldn't agree to get new cards printed – at least she realised that was a minor admin matter – but even though she'd now been using her new title around the office and on calls for weeks, she was worried that I wasn't serious enough about it to allow her to put it on business cards. Not a problem. Go ahead. But mine had to be changed too; my existing English ones had me down as a humble "Director". She insisted we put "President and CEO". Pretentious, unnecessary and over the top in my opinion, but I wasn't going to argue with her about it. It was a minor win I could let her have.

She was still looking nervous.

"Is that it?"

"No. I have something else to tell you and you will not like it."

"Try me."

"You have to shave off your beard. Facial hair is very rude in China."

That was a step too far for me.

"I won't do it. People will have to accept me as I am."

I've had a beard since I was 21. It wasn't something I'd planned; it wasn't a statement of fashion or rebellion. I'd simply forgotten to take a razor with me on a holiday, so it became an experiment. Then, with a week of stubble, I'd decided that rather than shave it off straight away, I'd wait another week or two and see how it looked then. My mother, who had always been scathing about men with beards and moustaches, saw me with it three weeks later, and shocked me by telling me it was an enormous improvement, and I should keep it! Was that because it hid my face? Anyway, I did keep it. Then, and ever since. It's changed length and colour over time, but never left my face even for a refurb. Every time I hear a comment about beards, I remember my mother. Sometimes one still reads or hears something about people not trusting men with beards, but I can't bring myself to believe that anyone intelligent would ever think that. And in Spain, where I have family and go frequently, beards were then the norm rather than the exception.

So, I wasn't going to shave it off now, and certainly not for Jin-Ae. Anyway, I wasn't sure she was right. I recalled pictures of Fu Manchu; didn't he have a beard, even if it was only a squiggly bit of hair down the middle of his chin?

As she left the meeting, looking upset and worried, she pulled a book from her bag and pushed it towards me across the desk.

"Read this before we go. You will see I am right, and you will learn many things."

It was a book on Asian business culture and etiquette.

True, the book did indeed say that facial hair was a no-no, but then went on to say that all the rules in the book only strictly applied to locals, and that foreigners were usually forgiven almost anything in the way of dress sense and appearance. I felt vindicated, but didn't think that Jin-Ae would accept that as justification. So, I stayed quiet.

Apart from the beard issue, she had once again impressed me with her sense of commitment and responsibility – but now I could see that she could have a difficult personality. Looking back, perhaps I should have taken more notice of the "you will see I am right" warning…

THE TRIP BEGINS
IN HONG KONG

It started well. My flight into Hong Kong was on time and uneventful, and I reached the hotel in the early evening, just as dusk was encroaching.

We were staying with a hotel chain where I had useful 'frequent guest' status. This meant that I (and a guest) had complimentary access to the Executive Lounge, even though I'd never been in that particular hotel before. The lounge was up on the 38th floor, from where there was a wonderful panoramic view of the harbour and city, all twinkling lights. Hong Kong is impressive at night. I called Jin-Ae to say I'd arrived, and to invite her to come up and meet me there. She'd arrived earlier in the day and told me she had been sleeping. Hardly surprising after a twelve-hour flight in economy.

Immediately on joining me, she said how impressed she was by the hotel; thank goodness for that! First doubt resolved. I think what made it for her was being able to come into the lounge where she could sit, queen of all she surveyed, cradling a cocktail complete with cherry and umbrella.

We had no meetings in Hong Kong; it was just a convenient place to meet, since we'd been coming from different places at different times. We wanted to arrive in Shanghai together; although I'd been to China before, that was many years earlier and for a holiday, so this was my first business visit, and the bureaucracy around getting a visa had made me more nervous than usual. Jin-Ae was travelling on a Korean passport and also seemed to be worried about the border controls, although she wouldn't tell me why. Anyway, by meeting up first in Hong Kong, we both had a night to get over the worst of jetlag, and for me at least a few hours the following morning to catch up with emails while she did a quick bit of sightseeing. By 2pm, we were leaving the hotel on our way to the airport for our flight to Shanghai.

Perhaps it was because some of her criticisms stung me back in London, or it was just that there was not much difference in the fare, but I'd booked business class for both of us for the flights between our three cities.

Why were we headed to Shanghai, and not Beijing or another Chinese city? Right from the start of the project, Jin-Ae had been most insistent that Shanghai was where the future was; it was the fastest-growing, most modern city, where everyone went and so that's where we should go too. I wasn't moved to argue with her, at least not about that.

Sitting on the Dragonair plane, she got out her file and took advantage of having my undivided attention for two hours to tell me more about the six companies we were going to meet with over the coming days. She'd chosen them as potential suitable partners for us, either for outsourcing or to create a new Joint Venture company.

It wasn't legally possible at the time to have a 100% owned foreign company in China; the maximum share for a company like ours was 50%, and for many types of business, the percentage was lower. That meant every foreign business was a joint venture, even if it didn't appear that way. So, even if the sign on the building was the name of a big foreign multinational, like HSBC or Citi, that didn't mean that they owned the operation; rather, they had a minority, or at best equal, shareholding with a Chinese company, and had licenced their name and intellectual property to the Chinese business. Our company was small, so we could aspire to the maximum 50%.

I'd made it clear to Jin-Ae back in January that she should look for companies we could work with who could do both customer support and data processing. I had only glanced at the list of names she had given me when we were back in London; none of them meant anything to me, so I just had to assume she had checked them out and that they fitted the criteria. Now she was explaining the capabilities of each, it was clear that she'd exceeded and deviated from her brief; she had also been looking for companies that could develop software for us.

It gave me a further insight into her attitude.

"We don't need any software development in China. We've already got a big operation in India," I told her.

"Yes, but they're no good. Not as good as the Chinese."

"Why do you say that? You know nothing about them."

"I met one of the Indian developers when he was in London. He was not modern. In Shanghai they are modern."

"None of our customers would trust us doing software development in China. They're famous for stealing IP and making copies of everything."

"That is a poor attitude! You must change! You must open your mind! You will see!"

Hmm. Well, indeed I would see. No harm in checking out their capabilities, I supposed, as long as they could also do the specific things we needed – data processing and customer support.

DAY 0
ARRIVAL IN SHANGHAI, CHINA

Jin-Ae's use of the term 'modern' proved not to be misplaced. Indeed, very apt. I found the Chinese to be fanatical about things being modern.

It started at the airport. Shanghai Pudong airport was certainly 'modern'. Huge and new. If first impressions count, these were good. I certainly remembered nothing 'modern' from when I had been to China before, on a short holiday to Beijing about 10 years earlier, in mid-winter. I remembered low, grey, functional buildings, and roads packed with bicycles despite the driving snow.

Getting the visa had been quite a bureaucratic hassle, so it came as some surprise to find that immigration was a breeze, even made entertaining (to me, anyhow) by the fact that the young officer who stamped my passport had a black goatee beard. So much for facial hair not being acceptable in China.

When we got outside, it was dark and pouring with

rain, so not a time to start sightseeing. However, even from the first few miles, looking out of the taxi windows, it was clear that things had either changed a lot since my last visit to China, or that Shanghai was indeed a different and 'modern' city. The taxi itself was modern (they're all VW Passats) too. However, one thing that definitely wasn't was the driver.

For once I'd not bothered to look at a map in any detail, so I had no concept of the route to the hotel. Unfortunately, neither did the driver or Jin-Ae, who, between them, kept up what sounded like a major argument for the entire journey. But then, to my untutored ear, every Chinese language conversation sounds like an argument.

All I knew was that our hotel was not in the main city centre but in Pudong, on the Eastern side of the river, supposedly the new scientific hub of Shanghai. The driver didn't have a map, and I had the feeling that even if he had, he wouldn't have known how to read it. China was modern enough to have mobile and data roaming, so my Blackberry worked, but the smartphone as we know it today wouldn't be launched on the world until the following year, so we had no GPS or online maps. I realised my error of not having printed out a map; I'd assumed that Jin-Ae would have done that, but no – like me, she'd assumed a taxi driver would know. The hotel name on its own wouldn't have helped; there are at least four or five Renaissance hotels in Shanghai. We had the address, but that wasn't any good without an up-to-date map; Shanghai was developing so fast that new streets were being created literally every day.

Eventually, we pulled up behind a police car. Jin-Ae got out to talk to the officers. Having stood in the pouring rain to get instruction, she returned to our cab wet and dripping, and now in an even worse mood than when she had left minutes earlier. With icy glare, she made the driver make a three-point turn in the middle of what looked like a six-lane motorway – admittedly with no other traffic on it – and go back in the direction from which we had come.

I could spot the hotel once we got near to it, since it was at least 30 floors high and had a big, illuminated sign on the top. I had difficulty in getting the attention of Jin-Ae and the driver, though, who were totally immersed in their argument, the driver insisting it was the wrong place and driving straight past. We got there in the end; none of us happy. But at least it was an impressive hotel. With a lounge and a bar. The latter much needed!

WEEK 1 - DAY 1
MONDAY IN SHANGHAI

The rain petered out overnight, and the following morning dawned bright and sunny. The view, both from my bedroom and the breakfast room, was of endless tower blocks, over a wide swathe of country, interspersed with fields and wide highways. The scale was vast. An immense city. All the buildings looked more or less identical, and most assuredly modern. The ones I could see were obviously residential; lines of washing hanging outside windows, especially when they're on the 50th floor, are a giveaway. I supposed that I was looking away from the city centre towards the outskirts – at least I hoped so, because if the commercial centre was beyond this view, we were a long way away from it.

I hardly recognised Jin-Ae when she arrived at breakfast; I'd taken no notice of what she was wearing before, but I suppose that, back in the office in London, she was always in unexceptional 'business casual'. Now she was dressed to impress, sporting a sharp pin-striped suit, obviously new, and very executive. She eyed me critically.

"Is that the only tie you have?"

"No, why?"

"There is a speck of grease on it."

And indeed there was, if only of microscopic proportion. I hadn't noticed it before, and doubted anyone else would during the day ahead, but I promised to change it before we went out. I assumed my shirt and suit passed muster, as they attracted no comment. Having addressed my attire, and extracted a promise to take more care of my appearance in the future, Jin-Ae embarked on what was to be the first of our daily morning briefings. In over 20 years of business travel, I'd never before travelled with someone so organised or who made such professional preparations; I was both impressed and humbled, as I realised that it was my fault that I'd never nurtured other employees to plan like this; up until then, I'd always done all my own advance planning.

Jin-Ae explained that our first meeting was going to be with a company formed by a team of young professionals who'd told her that they specialised both in customer service and software development, so she thought they would be ideal for us. We left in a cab, soon after breakfast. This time, the taxi driver seemed to know the address.

Were I to do the journey again now, I'd go by subway instead, but at that time Shanghai only had its first two lines operational. Within a very few years, it would have built what must be one of the world's largest and most comprehensive subway systems, certainly rivalling London. And the city needed it, because what Shanghai definitely already had was a major traffic problem. I know that Jin-Ae wouldn't agree; she'd want us to travel in a big black limo instead, not because we'd enjoy it more, despite the traffic delays, but because it would 'keep up appearances'. As you'll learn when reading forward, that wouldn't have helped us at all for the meetings we had in Shanghai that week.

When I had holidayed in Beijing a decade earlier, the streets had been packed with cyclists; here and now there were none. It appeared that everyone who could afford a car had bought one and was driving themselves to work. All the cars looked new; another reminder that the Chinese want everything to be modern. New cars, new roads, new buildings on either side. I'd never seen anywhere so overwhelmingly 'modern'. Despite the very wide highways, many of them built on stilts as overpasses which then tangled together at junctions like concrete snakes, nothing was moving at more than a crawl. There were just so many cars. I'd thought that the São Paulo rush hour was the world's worst, or maybe that was Cairo, but in those cities, even with a high proportion of 'old bangers' on the road, traffic moved faster than we were experiencing here.

Sitting in stationary traffic, however, gave me a lot of time to be wowed by the sights of the city. The view from the hotel had been towards the other direction, but almost as soon as we left and got on the first highway, the city centre came into view, with even higher buildings, all vying to be the most architecturally impressive. On approaching the river, the Oriental Pearl TV tower appeared; unique in style, with a tripod supporting a huge red and silver bulb, then a further three pillars supporting another one. These were quite unlike the space needles such as are found in cities like Adelaide, Las Vegas, Toronto and Seattle, all very similar to each other. People have remarked on buildings they liken to spacecraft from another planet: this one definitely qualifies for inclusion, being something along the lines of the Starship Enterprise meets the Eiffel Tower.

American city centres – quintessentially Manhattan – are packed with skyscrapers, many of them iconic, but a tourist riding in a taxi through downtown gets relatively little appreciation of the scale, however much one cranes one's neck. Shanghai not only has more space between buildings, but because the highways are elevated, even a jaded business traveller can be uplifted by fantastic and inspiring views of the city. Square buildings, pointy buildings, amazingly shaped buildings that appear to defy gravity, an octagonal one with what looks like a pineapple on the top, bronze mirrored ones, silver mirrored ones, a matt black one; the list goes on. Grand designs indeed.

As a first-time visitor to Shanghai, I couldn't stop looking; even after many more visits, with new high-rise buildings adding to the horizon each time, the cityscape has never ceased to impress me. At night, when it's all illuminated, it looks even more spectacular. So much so that for my future visits, I deliberately found a hotel on the Shanghai city side with a view over the river towards Pudong. I know that everything is government mandated, and the destruction of old quarters of the city has displaced tens if not hundreds of thousands of people; but as an outside observer, one can only be impressed by the Chinese: the vision of their architects, the ingenuity of city planners, and the sheer industriousness of the workers who construct these buildings with such incredible speed and skills. Perhaps that rapid rate of enterprise registers above all else. On later visits, when I stayed in the same hotel and ended up always with a room that, as well as presenting awesome night-time views, overlooked a construction site. On each occasion, I watched that building grow, starting from ground level, with another storey added every few days I was there. It climbed from foundations to sixty floors in the space of less than a single year. Back home, it's taken some builders just as long to get started on the first floor of a new house they're constructing at the end of my road.

The only sad thing was being witness to – well, almost – the destruction of the old architectures and communities. On my second stay in that hotel, I'd gone for an evening walk in a different direction than one I'd taken before, just for a change of scene. At first it was unpromising, but then I chanced upon a long street of old houses that had turned itself into a night food market. Instead of stalls in the street, the front rooms of the houses were kitchens and the owners, who I assumed lived upstairs or at the back, simply put up trestle tables in front to show and sell their wares. Crowded, ethnic – not another Westerner in sight – and packed with enticing smells and tasty, very cheap snacks. One could enjoy a gourmet feast as one wandered down the lane, nibbling a delicacy from one place while choosing another from the table outside the house next door. For my next visit, it was my must-go dining destination, but on the third it had completely disappeared, becoming just another building site. By the fourth, a gleaming new mall had taken its place. Obviously, the old street wasn't modern enough. I wonder still where the people went.

Back to my story: we'd been in the taxi for about an hour. It looked to me like we'd crossed the city centre and were headed out again on the opposite side. With no map or actual idea where we were going, I didn't much like the feeling of being out of control, but I'd relied on Jin-Ae to explain our destination to the driver. Unlike the one on the previous evening, coming from the airport, this one seemed quite certain of how to reach our destination. But clearly it wasn't in the centre, as Jin-Ae had said. It proved to be a long, long ride. I watched the taxi meter click ever upwards; the amount didn't look very much though, so I assumed that, as so often happens in cities around the world, we'd be presented on arrival with a conversion chart that would multiply the metered fare by at least three or four. But no, the meter was correct (the driver seemed most put out that I was questioning it), and the fare shown was the fare to be paid. About three dollars. A printed receipt for every journey. And no tipping.

The place at which we'd been dropped off didn't look like the offices of an IT company. Rather, it was a hairdresser's salon. My immediate reaction was that Jin-Ae had intentionally brought me here to get my beard shaved off and, coupled with the longer-than-predicted journey, I was feeling quite angry. But that wasn't it; Jin-Ae was worried too.

"The taxi driver says this is the right place and he wouldn't wait for me to check first."

It was an incongruous destination in other ways, best described as an old house with a ground floor shopfront to a hairdresser's, a building on its own, surrounded by modern towers. As I found out later, Shanghai was going through a phase where the government wanted to redevelop everything. Well, everything that wasn't modern. That meant pulling down all the older buildings, regardless of architectural merit, historic significance or whether or not anyone lived in them. In the rare cases where occupiers were successfully holding out against eviction, the government simply razed all the other buildings around them and built new ones, leaving – at least until all legal options ran out – the odd single old house still standing, like this one, overshadowed by modern 60-storey skyscrapers just yards away.

"Maybe they just gave you the block address, and it's one of the towers next door," I suggested.

Jin-Ae went into the hairdressers to ask. She returned quickly, beckoning me to the door. "It's the right address – they are at the back."

Unlikely as it seemed, indeed they were. Three young men in their twenties, modelling themselves on Japanese pop culture. That's now called *Harajuku*. All three were dressed in luminous fruit-drop coloured T-shirts (cerise, lime green and yellow, helping to tell them apart), torn jeans and braces. Appropriately, for their being based behind a hair salon, they sported spiky post-punk gelled black hair pointing out in all directions north, south, west and east. It was all fashion statement enough to make me feel old, out of place, and very much over-dressed in my formal suit and (clean) tie. Heaven knows what Jin-Ae was thinking; she might have been only a few years older than these guys, but her tastes struck me as even more conservative than mine.

The three young entrepreneurs were all seated around a table, eyes focused on their laptops. Judging from the boxes stacked against one wall, their office doubled as a store room for the salon.

Jin-Ae, who on the taxi ride over had been talking up this operation as a well-established software development house, was clearly embarrassed.

"I'm sorry, I'm sorry," she kept repeating in a hushed voice, even before we'd said anything much more than "hello" to our hosts.

"It's OK," I replied, "it's not the first time that something like this has happened to me."

Nearly a decade earlier, I'd gone to see a business in India that had been represented to me as a leading software development house, only to find that it was an ancient – and literally cobwebbed – former clothing factory in the middle of a slum. At least this setup was quite an improvement on that – firstly, they had computers, and secondly, whilst the access might be weird, it didn't feel unsafe. Additionally, I mused, if we ended up doing business here I could perhaps get myself a free beard trim whenever I visited.

Anyway, here we were. We'd come all this way, and I wanted to find out what these guys offered, even if our first impressions were to turn on our heels and go.

Jin-Ae chatted to the three of them briefly in Mandarin. "First, we must have tea."

Ah, the tea ceremony. No meeting in China starts without tea. One of the young men disappeared out the back and returned a minute or two later with two tea mugs. These are made-for-purpose and ubiquitous in China. They comprise a mug made of china (what else?) with a china strainer device, a bit like a second smaller cup with holes in its base, that sits on top of it. The tea leaves go into the top strainer, water is poured over and filters through into the mug. As the top device fits partly inside the mug below, one leaves it there to continue the brewing until content with the strength, then removes it and puts it onto its lid, that doubles as a saucer. All very scientific, and fascinating to observe.

Tea over, time for business.

"We are expert software developers," the spokesman, who introduced himself as Meng Yao, told me. "We can copy any computer game you like! Look, we are making here Chinese version of 'Grand Theft Auto'! What games do you want?"

"We don't want games. We want to develop specialist business software," I replied.

"It is all the same! We do anything!"

Meng Yao was so engaging, standing there and grinning broadly, that I couldn't bring myself to tell him that I didn't agree it was all the same, nor that we seemed to have just come across proof of what everyone was saying about the Chinese copying Western software.

Jin-Ae asked him about doing customer support for us.

"No problem! We do anything!"

His English wasn't so good but, thinking kindly, we didn't actually need that. What we would need was regional languages.

"Do you have anyone who speaks Japanese?"

"Yes! Bo here is fluent in Japanese!"

Jin-Ae turned to Bo and asked him something in what I assumed was Japanese. He looked completely blank, and answered her, in Chinese (she told me) that he didn't understand what she was saying. So, not fluent.

"No problem!" said Meng Yao. "We hire more people!"

Just then, I realised how thin the walls were. A noisy dispute had started in the hairdressing salon out front, and it sounded like objects were getting thrown around.

"Isn't it too noisy to concentrate here?" I asked. Jin-Ae translated.

"We expand! We have a lot more space!" Meng Yao proudly opened the back door, revealing a room with a sink piled with dirty cups – presumably where our tea had come from – against one wall, a lavatory pan against the other and more storage in between. He led us from there through another door into an empty room that made my cobwebbed clothing workshop in India look sophisticated. "We clean up! We modernise!"

Hmm, no, I don't think so. We made our excuses and left pretty quickly.

Jin-Ae was very subdued in the taxi, upset that she had failed with this first meeting. In hindsight, it was easy to understand how she had been 'had'. You don't have to talk for long to someone like Meng Yao on the phone, telling you how great everything is and how nothing is a problem, before you begin to believe the hype and think that his company must be an outstanding one. To her credit, she had asked for a reference, the contact details for somebody she could call and talk to about the company. The name she was given was probably the client for the 'Grand Theft Auto' clone, as he had been full of praise for Meng Yao and his team.

I hadn't dared ask why they had set up in a hairdresser's while we were there, but apparently Jin-Ae had. The hairdresser was his mother. Jin-Ae had concluded that it was almost certainly the ancestral home, and the family may well have lived upstairs. There was I thinking that in China everything was run by the government, and on our very first morning we'd chanced upon a real old-fashioned family-owned business.

Our next stop was to be the Great Wall Company. A name that immediately made me think of Chinese restaurants; I think I've seen a Great Wall restaurant in almost every city I've ever been to. Jin-Ae assured me that it was a software and services company, and that she had been told it was big and long-established. But first (and being reminded of restaurants) it was time for lunch; our meeting wasn't for another couple of hours.

The directions Jin-Ae had been given indicated that the office building where we were going was located opposite the railway station. Figuring that would be a good place to find somewhere to eat, Jin-Ae told the taxi driver to head for there. Shanghai railway station proved to be vast, with countless snack food and noodle stands all around the perimeter of the concourse. They all looked much the same; the only variation seemed to be how hygienic (or, better put, not too unhygienic) the stall and bowls appeared, and how fierce and off-putting its owner looked to be – invariably a very short old woman, in a pink or blue nylon housecoat, brandishing tongs in one hand and a ladle in the other.

Jin-Ae chose one of the stalls, I suppose on the logical basis that it looked to be the busiest. Soup noodles must be the most popular quick lunch in all the countries of southeast Asia; the chef, if I can stretch credibility enough to call her that, picks up and drops a tongs-full of either yellow (wheat) or white (rice) noodles in a bowl, adds a few leaves

175

or bits of cold meat or dumplings, and pours a ladleful of stock (closely resembling dishwater) from a cauldron over the top. That's your lunch.

I love soup noodles, particularly when they've got dumplings or won-tons (same thing but wrapped in fine pastry) and spicy sauce stirred into the stock, but ideally served by a waiter, at a nicely laid table, in a china bowl, with quality (or at least disposable) chopsticks and a clean soup spoon. Really, it's not snobbery. Soup noodles lose a lot of their appeal when one sees the individual ingredients in plastic buckets on a stall counter-top, then watches the dishing-up ceremony, and has them presented in a pink plastic bowl of questionable cleanliness, with old plastic chopsticks and a chipped ceramic spoon fished out of a washing-up bowl full of dirty water. But that was how it was meant to be; it was fun to be there, I was hungry, and a billion Chinese can't be wrong... can they?

We perched on stools at a trestle table alongside a dozen other diners, all of whom looked like men in a hurry, and joined in the fun of seeing who could be the noisiest and messiest slurper of soup noodles. Chinese in general are enthusiastic and noisy eaters and, according to the etiquette book that Jin-Ae gave me, slurping one's noodles is seen as a sign of appreciation. I joined in, anyway. Jin-Ae was being very ladylike, keeping her bowl at arm's length, picking up the noodles carefully with her chopsticks and waiting for the soup to drip off before moving her head over the bowl to eat the noodles. This meant she ate very slowly and, as a result, ate very little, leaving at least half of her portion; perhaps that was why she managed to keep so slim. Also, how she kept her new suit clean.

Sadly, I've always been a messy eater, regardless of the dish in front of me, and Jin-Ae admonished me for dripping soup onto my jacket. I was just surprised that I hadn't got it on my shirt (though I'd had the foresight, born from long experience, to carry a spare in my briefcase). That was her second criticism of my attire since we'd started this trip. It wouldn't be her last.

Nourished for the afternoon, and trusting that we wouldn't regret our lunch later, we set off in search of the Great Wall company offices. "Opposite the station" were incomplete and not entirely helpful directions when said station is vast and has exits on three sides, each leading to equally vast courtyards, beyond which lie elevated motorways and at least fifty buildings which could be described as being "opposite the station". Each of them a good ten minutes' walk from a station exit. Add twenty minutes of Jin-Ae animatedly asking the way of many people, and another twenty when we got it wrong and crossed the wrong road to the wrong building, and it must have taken an hour to find the right place. But once we did, it was at least a real office building, with an actual sign outside, a suitably impressive entrance hall and a receptionist.

Reassured, we awaited our host. He arrived and introduced himself as Lin. The contrast from the men we had met that morning couldn't have been more striking. Middle-aged, dressed in a black suit, white shirt, black tie, and with a very dour, serious expression, he looked more like an undertaker than a software developer.

Lin led us into a large open-plan office, divided by low partitions into cubicles. About 50 of them. Each was occupied by a man – they were all men – each also dressed in a black suit with a white shirt and black tie. All appeared to be working diligently, using tower computers with cathode ray screens of a type already obsolete in the West – green letters on a black background. I was reminded of Jin-Ae's assertation that Chinese software developers were 'modern'. Not these ones. The cubes were austere; grey partitions, grey desks, grey floor, no pictures, no trinkets. Surprisingly, not even a sheet of paper. No noise, except for the tapping of keyboards. This was serious stuff. And seriously dispiriting.

We were led on a long and extraordinarily repetitious guided tour of the office, moving from cube to cube, workstation to workstation. Each housing its funereal developer, tapping away, fixated on the screen in front of him, none being introduced to us, none acknowledging our presence. Lin explained each of their specialities and expertise – one a physicist, one a biologist, one a numerical analyst, and so on – getting as animated as an undertaker in charge of a Chinese software development team could be. He was at pains to point out how careful they were with confidentiality, that he couldn't tell us the actual projects that any of the team were working on, but no matter – what was on their screens was all in Chinese, so double Dutch, or the Asian equivalent, to me. Maybe Jin-Ae understood, but if she did, she wasn't letting on.

I'd been working with software developers in the West for twenty years; almost always dressed as casually as they can get away with, headphones on, surrounded by junk of one kind or another, some lurid-coloured caffeinated energy drink at hand, a buzz of activity. I'd often wondered how much real work ever got done, despite the team hugs and briefings, which in my opinion had more to do with American business fashion and convincing senior management that something useful was happening, rather than actually working more efficiently.

The Great Wall experience was a total contrast – and totally depressing. Nothing like an inspirational visit to the Great Wall itself. Lin was trying to sell their services in his own way, but the cultural void between us didn't help him. He wanted us to see a diligent, committed, efficient organisation. I just saw highly educated, skilled young men treated as modern slaves and chained to their desks in a sterile and minimalist prison.

The experience was set to become yet more surreal. The tour finally over, we were ushered into a conference room. As austere as the main office, this simply had a long, long table with a row of nine chairs ranged along one side. On the other, just two chairs in the centre, where we were instructed to sit.

Lin left the room for a few minutes, leaving us alone and looking at each other, both fearful to say a word in case we disagreed about something.

Lin returned, leading a procession of seven other men in black.

"Our management team."

We rose from our chairs and bowed at each other, Japanese-style. The eight of them sat on the opposite side of the table to us, leaving the middle chair empty. All looking at us, no-one speaking a word. A long minute later, a very short, rather elderly lady – also dressed in funereal black – waddled in and seated herself in the empty chair in the middle of the row, directly facing us. She smiled; well, she attempted to twist her mouth. Too much effort. Her expression reverted to seriousness. Lin, sitting next to her, now spoke and introduced her as the Managing Director. She didn't speak any English. Nor, it transpired, did any of the others – or if they did, we would never know, as either they weren't brave enough to try or were inhibited by the business hierarchy.

A scene that could have come out of Kafka. I've never felt so uncomfortable in a business meeting. Sitting opposite this row of eight men and one woman, all dressed identically in black, all with chillingly straight faces, gave me the impression of being on trial. I certainly didn't feel like the potential customer that I was. I just wanted to get out – but knew that I couldn't do that until arguments had been heard on both sides and judgement had been passed. I just had to hope for a not guilty verdict.

The MD spoke and Lin translated; words of welcome. I reciprocated and Jin-Ae translated. I turned to Jin-Ae. "Perhaps it would be better if you told them what we are looking for in Mandarin, so it doesn't need to be translated." She shook her head violently; this wasn't a place for a young woman to exist, let alone talk independently or demonstrate any ability above servility.

Once again, from my perspective, we were just going through the motions. I'd seen a side of Chinese business operations that I hadn't anticipated and had quickly concluded that we could not do business with them. Still, for politeness' sake, I had to tell them about our company, explain what we were looking for and ask useful and intelligent questions of the kind that I'd ask if I was seriously considering giving them work. It wasn't easy; the inquisition format was distracting and making me forget the reason I was there.

Somehow, though, I remembered our purpose and had an inspiration. All we'd seen were software developers. I explained that what I was specifically looking for was data processing and customer service operations.

I simply couldn't imagine any of the workers I'd seen in the main office doing either of those things. I was hoping that they'd say they were services they couldn't provide, and would give us an excuse to leave without either side losing face, that social necessity that's so critical in the East.

Lin discussed briefly with the MD, then turned and repeated the same words as I'd heard from Meng Yao in the morning. "No problem. We do anything."

I hadn't been convinced by Meng Yao, but at least he had bubbling enthusiasm enough to make me believe that, given the chance, he would try, and that he'd set a team up in the way we asked. Being told "No problem," by Lin in such a deadpan manner was worse. Especially as I simply wouldn't want them to try.

Fortunately, another doorway to escape opened. The MD got Lin to ask a question.

"How big is the project to translate all your software into Chinese?"

"We don't want it in Chinese. We only need our internet web pages translating; the software beneath it will all be in English," I told him.

"This is a problem. We do not work with the internet."

I'd thought the computers and the screens I'd seen looked primitive, but this proved it.

"We can copy all your code onto Chinese servers so that your customers here can use it," Lin ventured.

"I'm sorry. Our customers won't allow us to load their data onto Chinese servers. Ours are only in the USA and Germany."

"That is sad, we are only allowed to use Chinese servers."

That gave me proof – if any were needed – that Great Wall was government owned or controlled, but it didn't matter. It was what I required to terminate the meeting without either side losing face.

"Let us hope that the situation changes in the future and then we can talk again," I said. Contented nods all round. All standing. Deep bows.

We proceeded out of the conference room, two by two, me and the MD in front, Lin and Jin-Ae behind us, the management team following on. The MD turned to Lin and said something, a question that he translated.

"The MD wants to know how old you are."

Not a question I've been asked in business meetings before.

"Fifty-two."

"Ah, very old." Charming.

Hurried conversation with MD ensued.

"Our MD says you are even older than her. This means we have great respect for you."

Even though I'd read in the book that Jin-Ae had given me that the Chinese have great respect for age, this didn't make me feel very good. I didn't feel old, and certainly didn't want anyone to think I was old, and their MD looked like she was about 80! If she was actually younger than me (and I suspected that Lin only said this because he thought I would be happy) then these Chinese people age very fast, I thought.

Time to get out, back to the hotel and straight to the bar to drown the sorrows of my aged body!

Well, that's what I would have done had I been on my own, but I was with Jin-Ae, and she had different ideas. To her, crashing out at the end of a business day, or getting sloshed without first having a comprehensive post-mortem of our meetings, simply wasn't acceptable. I could hardly disagree; after all, we were there on a serious mission, she was the one who had researched the companies and set up the meetings, and I needed her to understand how seriously I was taking this.

That didn't mean that we couldn't go to the bar and have a drink though; except we didn't need to. We could go to the hotel's Executive Lounge instead. Ah, the joys of loyalty to my favourite hotel chain! Despite the nose-to-tail snail's pace journey back to the hotel, there was still an hour of the complimentary early evening cocktail session left, and the so-called "hors d'oeuvres" left out for our delectation were better in quantity and quality than many a paid-for hotel buffet dinner. In the USA, where the chain is headquartered, the catering is meagre; just a few pre-packed snacks, and you have to pay for the alcohol. Elsewhere, though, especially in the Far East, there's really no need at all to go anywhere else for dinner. Countless business travellers stay with the same chain for that reason, maintain enough loyalty points to ensure lounge access, and park themselves there all evening, in whichever hotel and city that may be.

So we had a variety of freshly steamed dim sum dumplings, spare ribs in black bean sauce, pork buns, and little dishes of vegetables sauteed with garlic and ginger. Even bowls of noodles. And help yourself to wine.

To Jin-Ae this was a novel experience, and one she liked very much. I suspected that, despite what she'd told me in London, these were the first nights she'd spent in five-star hotels. I'm guessing she also thought that all hotels of that grade were the same and that all guests got the same treatment.

Even if Day One had proved to be totally futile from a business perspective, I was happy; I had at least had new, interesting and amusing experiences and learnt something of Chinese business practices.

I was sanguine because I'd had plenty of unsuccessful meetings with inappropriate people; but Jin-Ae was distraught about the way the day had gone. She too had realised how impossible the young men in the morning had been, and though we hadn't talked in the taxi coming back, she knew also that I was negative about the afternoon's Great Wall meeting, but I wasn't sure whether she shared the same concerns or whether in her mind it was OK, and she was blaming me for not adapting to Chinese business culture. Now all she could say was "sorry" over and over again, averting her eyes and looking down into her lap.

Either way, I think she was expecting me to be angry with her for a wasted day. I told her that wasn't the way I saw it. The meetings had actually taught me a lot. They'd revealed two totally contrasting Chinese business cultures, neither of which I could have guessed at from anything I'd heard before I came, let alone from the book on business etiquette that she'd given me to read back in London. Despite the 'chalk and cheese' variations, in both offices I'd seen a commitment to hard work, even if they'd come with attitudes totally alien to me.

My main conclusion was not that these companies couldn't do the job; rather, that I thought they would simply be impossible to work with.

There's actually an advantage in the first meetings in any unfamiliar country being a failure, and spending time with people you quickly realise you'll never do business with. You discover what makes people and businesses tick; you see things and ways of working you don't like and, in doing so, come to realise some of the things you value most that you've never thought very clearly about before.

Those lessons mean you can start Day Two with at least a little real experience under your belt; not yet a pro, but not a rookie either.

I'd also enjoyed the experience of being driven through Shanghai, seeing the amazing constructions, completed and in progress, first by day, and then being wowed by the light show of the night, played out on those same buildings, and totally transforming the vista on the way back to the hotel. Seeing the miraculous things that humankind can create never fails to lift my spirits!

Jin-Ae cheered up totally when I told her this, changing completely from "I am sorry I let you down," to "You see, I always told you how important these meetings were." Maybe I shouldn't have let her know my thoughts; after that, I never heard or saw again even the tiniest touch of humility from her.

If I'd been uncertain before whether she thought that my dislike of Great Wall was my fault or theirs, now she was unreservedly on my side. I still wasn't sure of her sincerity; I'm always watching out for people who tell me what they think I want to hear. In all truth, I hate that, even though

I'm not immune to a little judicious flattery once in a while. Generally, I want people to be honest with me, however uncomfortable it might make me feel. But since by now I'd had a couple of glasses of wine, and lost count of the dim sum dumplings I'd eaten, I was past caring about whether it was flannel or sincerity I was getting from Jin-Ae. So, sated and having had more than enough of each other's company, we parted off to our rooms. In my case, to catch up with the rest of the world via email; it might be evening in Shanghai, but it was lunchtime in London, early morning in America. Lots to read and reply to. And the messages were still coming in.

WEEK 1 - DAY 2
TUESDAY IN SHANGHAI

The two meetings that Jin-Ae had arranged on our second day reassured me that yes, there were professionally managed companies that could do part or all of what we needed. I wasn't inspired by either, but I learnt a lot more about Chinese business culture, and I was beginning to appreciate the positives. The most important business of the day was yet to come, though.

China is infamous as a source of fake designer goods, and Jin-Ae had found out where there was a market that sold them. I didn't need any convincing to agree to go there after our afternoon meeting on Tuesday; although I didn't want to buy anything, I like markets, and knew it would be entertaining to experience one in China. For Jin-Ae, though, there was a serious purpose to the mission. She wanted a Gucci handbag. A quality fake, she said, that had to be cheap but indistinguishable from the real thing.

We got a taxi to drop us at the entrance. It didn't look to be a very salubrious neighbourhood. A high wire mesh fence separated the open-air market from the road, and on all other sides, as far as I could see, were old, disused, and partly demolished buildings. It was getting dark, and there were shady-looking characters standing by the market entrance, two or three of them trying to force themselves on us as 'guides'. Jin-Ae's immediate reaction was to try to hail a taxi to leave – now we'd got here, she was scared, and didn't want to go in.

Maybe it was because I'd walked round much rougher markets and neighbourhoods in many other cities, but this place didn't look particularly risky to me. There were certainly some apparent down-and-outs hanging around, but they looked to be outnumbered by various uniformed men, either police or security. I told her I was going in anyway, and she could leave if she wanted. I'd definitely be no good if faced with robbers or hoodlums, but my decision was enough to give her some confidence, and she followed me in. There were a lot of stalls with all kinds of clothing, but very few customers.

The sight of a westerner got the stallholders very excited, and most of them tried to pull us in to see their wares. I wasn't intending to buy anything, but lingered to look at a display of silk ties. I like wearing ties. They all had labels like Versace, Ermenegildo Zegna, Burberry and Lanvin. They looked exactly like the real thing, even though I didn't believe the 'Made in Italy' labels sewn on to them. I'd normally not spend much – my wardrobe is all chain store – but, unusually, had splashed out about £70 for one of those silk designer ties in a Heathrow Airport shop just a few months before, when I'd realised I'd forgotten to pack any for another trip I was making. So, I knew how much the real thing cost in London. The stall holder told me that any of her ties would cost 100 renmimbi – about £10. Just for the entertainment value of bargaining, and with no intention of buying, I offered 20 RMB – and, since I'd started haggling, ended up buying several at 30 RMB each, about £3. At that price I could have bought more than 20 for the price of just one tie in London. And they were extremely good ties; I'm not sure who would be able to tell the difference. Maybe they're not fakes.

Jin-Ae was impressed, especially as I'd let her choose the colours and it meant I could wear clean ties for the rest of the trip, at least until I spilt food or drink on them. But we hadn't gone to the market to buy ties for me; we were there because she wanted a Gucci handbag at Topshop prices. We set off in search of a handbag seller. There were plenty.

She found one that she liked, and it seemed she'd made a bargain as she started reaching for her purse. She'd been talking Mandarin with the guy, so of course I was in the dark.

"How much does he want?" I asked.

"Five hundred renmimbi, that's fifty pounds," she replied.

"That's ridiculous! Much too much." I had no idea how much any handbags cost, never mind Gucci, but it was clear from my tie negotiations that this market worked like most around the developing world.

Without asking her permission, I took over the bargaining. When it comes to price negotiation, every market trader everywhere in the world is fluent in English.

Not to mention whatever other language the prospective customer wants to converse in.

A minute or two later, the poor stallholder was telling us he was "suffering" but convinced that much luck would be coming to his family by making his first sale to an Englishman, so would agree "just this once" to a deal at 200 RMB – about £20. Jin-Ae was thrilled. In an unguarded moment, she said how glad she was that she had a "strong man" with her. That proved to be the only compliment I ever got from her, and the only time anyone has ever said that I am strong!

Shopping spree successfully completed, it was time for dinner, and Jin-Ae, in what I suppose was a celebratory mood, decided we should find a restaurant to try Shanghai Hot Pot. Determined on the menu, but having no idea of where to go, she gabbled at a taxi driver, seeking a recommendation. Maybe that works in a city like New York or London, but I don't think most drivers in Shanghai would have an opinion worth relying on; in this case, though, he was at least resourceful, and delivered us to a vast shopping mall where there were dozens of restaurants. I suppose his idea was that we would be bound to find whatever sort of restaurant we wanted there, and he was right.

My concept of hotpot up to then had been of the Lancashire variety, in other words a stew, and, since the only such regional dishes I had ever had in England were at school dinners in the wrong county, not appetising. So Shanghai Hot Pot was a revelation. It is indeed a pot, and it is hot, but that's where the similarity ends.

It's clearly a meal ceremony suited to larger groups than just the two of us, since they seated us at a large round table and took six chairs away, leaving just the two of us, staring at each other at a great distance across the divide. In between us lay a big circular well – the pot, made of metal with a central vertical sheet dividing it into two sections. Waiting staff arrived bearing huge jugs of boiling stock that they poured into the two sides; plain and dishwater-coloured on one, spicy and orange on the other. A heating element under the pot keeps the liquid simmering.

The menu handed to us was a single large plastic laminated sheet, scuffed and sticky. I hoped the food would prove more hygienic than the menu. On it were displayed pictures of plates of sliced raw meat, seafood, vegetables and noodles. I had to rely on Jin-Ae to read the adjacent words; all that leapt out to me, since I could understand the numerals, was that one plate of sliced meat cost about £5 whilst another that looked identical cost £50.

"I'm leaving you to order," I told her. "I trust you not to choose the most expensive items."

She didn't see that as a joke, which was how I'd intended it. The merit marks she had awarded me for negotiating for her handbag were deducted instantly. She glared at me, pure vitriol in her eyes. "I know you are mean. This is not the time to show off to me how rich you are." Oh my god, what might I have started now? Fortunately, there was a waiter standing by, and she turned away from me and gabbled furiously at him. Who knows what was said, but he disappeared and then returned a few minutes later, bearing several plates of raw ingredients.

"These are not the cheapest, but they are good enough for you to start with. Maybe when you appreciate the good things better, you will put your money where your mouth is." Jin-Ae hath spoken. Let me pray that we can now eat our hotpot in peace.

Her previous words left hanging, she now instructed me on how to eat hot pot. I paid close attention for fear of getting it wrong and fomenting a major scene. Another waitress arrived with a trolley laden with an array of pots containing a variety of coloured pastes and powders, looking for all the world like open paint tins. The idea is to choose various pastes – sesame, black bean, chilli, ginger and so on – and spices, flavours of which appeal and that you think will go together. The waiter spoons some of each of the ingredients you point to into a bowl and mixes them together to create your own recipe condiment. Unintentionally weird concoctions are, of course, quite feasible, but I was happy with my choice.

Then, with your chopsticks, you pick up a raw morsel – thinly sliced meat, prawns, sliced fish, and various vegetables – drop it into one side or other of the hot pot, according to your preference, leave it swimming for a few minutes until cooked, fish it out again, dip into your unique condiment and enjoy! This all requires some dexterity with chopsticks and bravery at holding them just a few centimetres above boiling stock. Once satisfied, or more to the point when all the raw ingredients you ordered have either been eaten or lost in the depths of the pot, you ladle some of the stock, now well-flavoured, over a bowl of noodles, and slurp contentedly until sated. Very tasty and, when experienced in a larger group surrounded by faces friendlier than Jin-Ae's that evening, very enjoyable too.

WEEK 1 - DAY 3
WEDNESDAY IN SHANGHAI

For our first meeting the following day, we were picked up at our hotel by the official driver of the company we were going to visit. I now found out that Jin-Ae hadn't agreed to this until she'd seen for herself that our hotel was sufficiently impressive. I'm not sure why it was important to impress the driver, but never mind. The only thing that stopped him from being recognisable as a chauffeur was the lack of a uniform and peaked cap, but it was obvious from first sight that he'd have liked to have had those. Unusually rotund for a Chinese man, he opened the door to the well-polished BMW and stood to attention as we got in, no doubt thinking this would impress us. I suppose that although the streets were full of new cars, there weren't so many of them that were upmarket European ones. Jin-Ae told me that we should call him Mister Ling.

Mister Ling, although clearly missing his peaked cap, held himself erect with arms stiffly poised over the steering wheel as he navigated us into the heart of Shanghai. I stared out of the window. It was the same view as yesterday and the day before, but not one I thought I would tire of easily.

It wasn't a long journey today; for some reason there was little traffic and no hold-ups, so after not much more than twenty minutes we stopped on a street corner in front of a Pizza Hut and a McDonalds. Mister Ling opened the door to let us out, and we were met on the pavement by our host, who shook our hands very effusively and introduced himself as Donald.

Donald seemed a very un-Chinese name. Although it hadn't been the case with the people we'd met on the previous two days, I was now to learn that many Chinese, and most of those who deal with Westerners, adopt and use English names, at least for business purposes. On later occasions, I found myself meeting many who had chosen extremely unlikely and sometimes downright hysterical names. I still remember interviewing a girl who came in and said, "my Chinese name is Yin, but my English name is Charming Darling". It was difficult keeping a straight face and taking an interview seriously after that…

Fortunately, Donald's office wasn't behind either of the fast-food restaurants; this was a 20-storey tower block, and the main entrance was between the two. His office was on floor 15, and we entered it to find a hive of activity; this environment was going to be much easier to relate to. We were led into a meeting room, with a round table, and invited to sit where we liked – no formality, thank goodness – and brought tea (of course). Donald spoke pretty good English; he was the owner of the business and told us that they already provided customer support services for other companies. It seemed like they did exactly what I was looking for – and Donald wasn't trying to sell us software development. In fact, he apologised – unnecessarily – for not having a development team or even understanding what they might do.

For reassurance, I asked to see staff doing the things he'd talked about. No problem! We walked around the office and watched work in progress. I grabbed an opportunity to tell Jin-Ae that this was exactly the sort of operation I was looking for, as I thought she'd be happy to hear that after the previous two days' lack of success.

"I knew that you would like this one, that is why I chose it."

Ah well, I thought, did you choose the ones yesterday and the day before because you knew I wouldn't? So much for my trying to give her a bit of credit.

After the tour, Donald insisted on taking us for lunch – at the Pizza Hut downstairs. American fast food was then a novelty in Shanghai and considered very upmarket. They hadn't only brought American pizza to China, they'd brought the prices too, so it must certainly have been a luxury that the average worker couldn't afford, perhaps proven by our being the only diners. Frankly, I'd rather have had Chinese food, but Donald's enthusiasm for pizza and things Western was very fetching, and I appreciated the gesture.

We had one more company to visit that afternoon; the last of the six that Jin-Ae had chosen. They did seem competent enough, but in retrospect, I think that I'd been so happy to find that Donald's company could do what we wanted that I'd lost interest in considering any alternatives. I terminated the meeting as quickly as politeness demanded, and as soon as we got out of the door, I told Jin-Ae that I'd made up my mind, and we should go with Donald. First, though, I wanted to go back and meet him again because I had a lot more questions if we were going to do business with him. She phoned, and he insisted that we come over straight away, which suited us fine. To say that he was thrilled he was going to get our business was an understatement, even though I was at pains to remind him that it was only going to be enough work to occupy two people. He insisted that we all go out to dinner together to celebrate.

Mister Ling was summonsed to drive us to the hotel and instructed to wait while we dropped our things and freshened up. Half an hour later, Jin-Ae appeared in the lobby, transformed from her sharp business suit, and now in a rather lurid long, reflective, dark blue dress. As usual, I hadn't bothered to change for a business dinner – I figured that Donald wouldn't have either – and felt a momentary pang of shame.

"I'm sorry, I don't have any better suit to dress up in," I told her

"It wouldn't matter. It wouldn't make you look any better."

With that, I knew that her past deference to me had now completely evaporated. Fine by me.

As we drove, Jin-Ae quizzed Mister Ling, and learnt that our dinner destination was the Old Railway Station. That didn't sound like a restaurant to me, but apparently it was. Hopefully not a McDonalds. In any case, I assumed that we weren't going to end up slurping noodles at a stall in an actual railway station; already been there, done that. We drove through the bright lights of downtown Shanghai and pulled up in front of a building that was definitely old, at least by Shanghai standards, but didn't look anything like a railway station. Going in, and finding ourselves in a long corridor with old pictures hanging on the wall on each side, the interior didn't look like a railway station either.

Donald was already there, waiting for us at the entrance, and explained that, in fact, it was actually an old convent. The main dining room had high windows along the length of the wall, facing onto an illuminated courtyard occupied by two old railway carriages. Quite how they got there, heaven knows; they certainly didn't come along tracks. A waiter led us down another corridor and up a ramp into one of the carriages, which must originally have been a dining car, and seated us in a compartment at the end.

"Have you tried Shanghai cuisine?" asked Donald.

"I'm not sure," I replied. "I'm very fond of the Chinese food that I have eaten, though."

"Ah, if you ate in England you will have had Hong Kong food, Cantonese. Shanghai cuisine is different, much better!"

I told him that I was looking forward to it, and we both said we were happy for him to order; Jin-Ae had reminded me that etiquette meant that the host ordered for the table. How brave we were! The menu was a large, thick, leather-bound tome. Ordering took ages, well, at least ten minutes. I wasn't sure whether it was just because Donald was leafing back and forth through the menu and asking lots of questions of the waiter, or if he was ordering a ludicrous number of dishes, but Jin-Ae presumably understood and didn't seem too worried.

The waiter returned with a carafe of what looked like water, except for the fact that it was in a beautiful glass bottle and was given great reverence when placed it in the centre of the table, together with three shot-sized glasses.

"First, we toast!" exclaimed Donald, pouring the liquid. We raised our glasses and I followed Donald's example by tipping it back in one.

I'd guessed it was vodka or something like it, but firewater would be a more accurate description. In fact, the only possible description. It tasted of nothing at all but burned the throat like battery acid (I'm guessing here, as I've never tried drinking acid of any sort).

"This is special Shanghai *Baijiu*," said Donald, proudly. "There are many kinds, many bad ones. This one is special, you will feel good!"

Unwisely, I accepted another. Now I could taste something, and yes, I did feel better. So, another. I wondered what the alcohol content was; it must have been very high. It didn't matter what food came now; I'd had the anaesthetic and my taste buds had been stripped clean.

It is really not a great idea to get drunk at business dinners, whether you're selling or buying, especially not the first one with a new contact that one doesn't know well. Fortunately, I think I stopped in time. Soon enough, anyway, to savour and remember my first experience of Shanghai cuisine.

And what an experience. Forget sweet and sour, forget chicken with cashew nuts, forget kung pao beef and dishes like those. Well, don't forget them completely, because you might well enjoy them more than some of the Shanghai delicacies we were introduced to.

First was Fish Head Soup. Yes, it's exactly as described. It arrived in a very wide, shallow bowl, filled with clear stock, with a dozen or more fish heads floating in it. As Donald demonstrated, a diner should pick up a fish head with chopsticks, put it whole in one's mouth, suck the flesh from the bone (noisily, of course, to show appreciation) and return the skeleton to the plate, after which one sups a spoonful of the fish broth. The flavours are delicate; although pleasant enough, I decided that one orders this for the experience rather than the taste. Or perhaps, if one is Chinese and entertaining innocent Westerners, to shock their senses. OK, I'm game for anything. I stole a glance at Jin-Ae; she may have been Chinese herself, but she looked fairly uncomfortable. I suppose it's not a dish that a well-dressed cultured young woman would choose; it's certainly not one that can be eaten delicately and with decorum.

A number of different dishes were brought to the table, but not as many as I'd speculated on from the length of the ordering process. An interesting mix of cold and hot dishes, all shared, all indeed different from Cantonese cuisine. Not dishes I might have ordered myself, but adventurous and very enjoyable. Not in any logical order; most Chinese food is just sent from the kitchen to the table when it's ready. Cold jellyfish. Hot crispy pork skin. Cold green beans. Hot sliced snake in black bean sauce. You get the idea.

Then, the table was cleared for what we were told would be the highlight of the meal; a dish that Donald told us was entitled "Goose Three Ways".

Two dishes were set in the centre of the table – Way One: the gizzards, and Way Two: the lower bony part of the leg with the foot attached. I'm not much of a lover of offal, and although I ate some gizzards and complimented

Donald, that offering didn't convert me. On next to Way Two. I followed Donald's example, picked up a leg with chopsticks and sucked it, getting a mouthful of not very much, all gristle. "Very delicious!" declared Donald. "Eat more! I can order more!"

I assured him that I'd had so much else to eat that just one of Way Two was enough. In any case, I had to leave space for Way Three.

The waiter placed a covered bowl in front of each of us, much deeper than a normal soup bowl, and removed the lids, revealing each to be full of stock with one whole goose leg swimming in the liquid. As instructed, we held out our hands for the waiter to put plastic gloves on them. The idea is that you plunge your gloved hands into the soup bowl, pull out said goose leg, and then munch at it, plunging and recovering the leg after each bite so as to pick up the juices from the broth. I like finger food as much as the next person, but this was the first time that I had eaten dinner with plastic gloves on.

I can't say that it wasn't fun, because it was; it just seemed a shame to me, as a bit of a foodie, that all this rigmarole wasn't justified by the flavours. Texture there was, yes; but, even after many subsequent visits to China, I never gained any enthusiasm for goose, duck or chicken feet and legs, with greasy, crunchy scales and gelatinous cartilage. I love fish, but I'd rather eat it off the bone with cutlery or even with chopsticks, rather than suck the heads, risk a mouthful of bones and wonder what was done with the other parts of the poor creatures. Goose leg is delicious, but I'd enjoy it more if eaten off a plate with a knife and fork and with a side plate of soup.

Jin-Ae, though, seemed to be used to all this, and certainly showed herself to be an aficionado of Way Two, the feet and legs.

Her polite appreciation was eclipsed by Donald's gung-ho enthusiasm, every bite or sup followed by an exclamation of "Very delicious!". I smiled, nodded, and tried to reciprocate as best I could.

"You will come back in September! We will have Hairy Crab season! Very delicious!"

"And you will stay for Moon Cake festival! Very special! Moon Cakes very delicious!"

Having indeed returned in September, not only in that year but others afterwards, I can confirm that hairy crabs are indeed delicious. It's the one other dish I've had that's eaten wearing plastic gloves. The crabs, apparently pulled from the mud in the bottom of the Shanghai river and simply steamed, are about 10cm across the shell. They come to the table in pairs, each crab chopped in half; one dips the open part in a light soy-based sauce and sucks out the meat, eating quite a lot of shell (fortunately soft) in the process, then continuing in the same way with the claws.

Moon cakes have a festival of their own in early October. There are at least two mythical stories about the origin of their name and, as you might expect, the moon is a central theme of both. The festival is not actually about the moon cakes – it's called the mid-Autumn festival – but it might as well be, as everyone I met in Shanghai talks about nothing else at that time of year. Personally, I don't find them exciting. They're basically just rather large spongy biscuits, about 10cm in diameter and 4cm thick, hence big enough to cut into segments but too small to classify as a cake, at least in my opinion. They're made of a rather dense and sickly sweet sponge wrapped around an even sweeter filling made of bean paste, with, at the core – and this is the critical component – a salted duck's egg. I don't have a very sweet tooth, and they are incredibly sweet.

What hairy crabs and moon cakes have in common is that they are both eye-wateringly expensive. I can't imagine that the average Chinese worker could afford either, but they're considered great delicacies, so they probably do enjoy them on very special occasions. They're also both, in season, on sale to travellers at Shanghai airport, the moon cakes always gift-wrapped in very decorative red boxes and the crabs packed in polystyrene foam boxes to keep them cool en route. They're sold from what look like ice cream trollies, parked right by the gates. The queues to buy them are long, as I once found out standing in what I mistakenly thought was a line to board my flight back to London.

Dinner over, Donald asked what our plans were for the next day, Thursday. I told him that we had nothing arranged; I'd told Jin-Ae not to arrange anything for Thursday or Friday so that we could go back to any company that had interested me, and also to give me time to catch up with emails and calls from our home base and other offices. So I said that, if Donald had the time, I'd like to sit down with him and confirm arrangements and costs for how we could work together in the future.

"Of course! But we must make the day very nice for you! We will go to the village! You will see old China! We can talk there!"

It was an attractive idea; the forecast was for continued fine spring weather, and I fancied sightseeing more than sitting in my hotel room and working on my own.

WEEK 1 - DAY 4
THURSDAY; A BUSINESS MEETING IN AN ARTIFICIAL VILLAGE

Mister Ling came to the hotel to pick us up after breakfast. Donald was with him. "Very fine hotel!" he exclaimed. I checked that Jin-Ae had heard him; she looked relieved.

Donald told us that we were going to a village called Zhujiajiao. I discovered later that this is one of a dozen 'touristic old villages' near Shanghai.

Getting there took an hour's drive through a flat landscape, mainly paddy fields, but for most of the journey I could see bunches of high tower blocks on the horizon, in whichever direction I looked. Eventually they petered out, and we drove through open countryside, finally arriving in Zhujiajiao. It was certainly a contrast to Shanghai; a small town with waterways, ancient bridges, and traditional old-style single-storey stone houses with curly-tiled roofs. And tourists. Lots of tourists. Every street seemed to be blocked by tour buses, and every pavement packed with tour groups, all of them Chinese, led by guides differentiated only by the colour of their umbrellas. The complicating factor that many of the women tourists were also carrying umbrellas, used as sunshades, made every tourist procession look both colourful and confusing.

Donald led us along streets and over bridges, all the time exclaiming, "Look how old!", "Very historic!" and so on. It was pretty, but didn't look very historic to me; in fact, quite 'modern', more like a Chinese Disneyland without the rides. I was even less convinced of any genuine history by the restaurant, where Donald had booked a private room so we could "do business" and eat lunch at the same time. If it were in England, it would be called Ye Olde Chinese Village Inne or something similarly quaint and ghastly. The walls were stone, but the timber beams were actually plastic, and just stuck on for show. To prove it, one such beam that had fallen off had simply been propped up in a corner, revealing itself to be faux.

Still, it made for a different day out which we would not have managed if left to our own devices, and we got all necessary business done. I decided it would be easy to work with Donald, though by the time we got back to the hotel I'd had quite enough of his company for the day. It would have been nice to have just relaxed over a glass of wine in the lounge, but Jin-Ae had other ideas, and insisted on doing a post-mortem of the entirety of the past week in Shanghai.

In her opinion, the key take-away was that she had done an amazing job in lining up the meetings, demonstrating how useless five of the six were, which went to prove that the sixth (Donald's company) was wonderful, and that I would never have known that if I hadn't spent many hours visiting the others. It was clear that she was expecting me to compliment her on how wonderful she was. I was reluctant to praise too highly, as even though she had certainly worked hard and found one good candidate company, I could guess where this was heading. She was good, but far from perfect, and I was finding her increasingly irritating. With almost two more weeks to go, I certainly didn't want her feeling invincible. But I must have said something to her satisfaction, as she rewarded me by going and bringing me a glass of wine from the buffet table, unsolicited.

WEEK 1 - DAY 5
FRIDAY IN SHANGHAI

Any hope of a good 'morning in the office' evaporated at breakfast. Jin-Ae got a phone call and jabbered away quite excitedly, for long enough for me to concentrate on enjoying my third cup of coffee.

"It is wonderful news! We go to Shanghai government office today! We meet minister!" she gushed.

The call had been from Donald. Jin-Ae relayed the news that he'd been talking with the Minister of Energy for the Shanghai Province, who he claimed was a very good friend of his (over the coming months, I learnt that Donald claimed to be a very good friend of countless men of questionable power and influence).

"Minister is very interested in the work that we do. It is very high priority for Shanghai Government!" she went on.

This was a bit surprising, as we hadn't told Donald a great deal about our business, and when I had talked him through our standard presentation on Wednesday, I hadn't even been sure that he was paying much attention. I supposed Jin-Ae had told him more.

"We must prepare special presentation now!" she insisted.

"Does the minister understand English?"

"No, you will prepare the presentation in English, and I will translate."

"What time is this meeting?"

"Mister Ling will come for us at 10.30." OK, so we had an hour or thereabouts.

She opened her laptop and pulled up the standard presentation we'd been showing our potential partners all week. About twenty slides. Far too many.

"I think we only need five or six," I said. "I am sure the minister will only have a very short time for us. Anyway, we have no time to prepare."

I picked a few and Jin-Ae rushed off to her room to do the translation. That gave me time to reply to the most urgent emails. I'd not make any dent in my backlog, but going to see a Chinese government minister, even if only one for the region of Shanghai, was an intriguing prospect. Frankly, I've never had much time for government people in my own country or anywhere else; of the ones I've met, the politicians always seemed to be self-important, in a terrible hurry and not seriously interested in anything anyone says or shows them, and the civil servants were nonentities. But then, I've never met ones with genuine influence, or said the right things, or voted the right way, or was a member of the right club, or went to the right school, or played golf, or done any of the other things that middle-aged self-made businessmen often do. Not that these factors had ever concerned me. I'd managed to build a business with zero help from my own government, and felt happier for that. Almost all the government people I had met in my life were British. Here was an opportunity to be in the company of a Chinese minister. It might not achieve anything, but we had the time, and this had to be an experience worth having.

Mister Ling had obviously polished the car again since yesterday and been told to look smart. He drove us into the centre of Shanghai. I'd assumed we'd be going to some ordinary-looking office block, but no, we pulled up in front of a genuinely old (for Shanghai) pillared and porticoed building that wouldn't have looked out of place in Athens. Donald was waiting for us on the pavement and led us up the steps to the front entrance. No red carpet outside, and none expected; but lots of red carpet in the lobby, a huge, tall space with stone walls and a high painted ceiling, ringed by antique-style chairs with gold-painted curly arms and red cushions. There must have been fifty or more such chairs, but we were the only people there, apart from a young functionary who pointed us to which ones we should sit on, and then promptly disappeared.

Fifteen long minutes later, he reappeared, beckoning us to follow him into an even larger space adjacent to the lobby. This massive room was very grand in every sense; just as high a ceiling, red carpet, floor-to-ceiling windows facing the street outside, elaborate plaster mouldings on the ceiling and around the windows. Versailles comes to Shanghai. This room was ringed by armchairs; not upright wooden ones like in the lobby, but deeply upholstered real armchairs. Lots of them, placed all around the walls;

nothing at all in the centre of the room. We were instructed to sit on one side.

Within a minute of our settling, the minister strolled into the room flanked by two aides. We stood again and bowed at each other, then all sat once more. So here we all were in armchairs – them on one side of the room, us on the other, with ten metres of space between us. Donald introduced me and Jin-Ae in Mandarin, and there then began an extremely stilted conversation.

The minister said something to one of his aides, who got out of his armchair, scuttled across to me, and said in English:

"The minister says you are very welcome in Shanghai, and he hopes that you will do good business here."

"Please tell him that we are very grateful to be welcomed by him and we look forward to being very successful here," I replied.

Aide duly scurried back across the floor, sat next to the minister and, presumably, translated what I said. He returned with another message:

"Donald is trusted businessman. You will do good business with him."

"Thank you for saying that. We look forward to working together."

Aide scurried back again, relaying my message. This rigmarole went on for about ten minutes; nothing whatever of any purpose being said by either party, but lots of smiling and nodding by the principals, and a lot of exercise for the junior aide.

I had to assume that he was actually translating what we were saying. For all I know, the minister could have been asking something else altogether and the aide could have been making up the replies…

"Ask him what he had for dinner last night."

"He says he had the sea cucumber with fried rice. It was very bland."

"Tell him if he had taken chilli sauce with it that would have been better. He must return for Hairy Crab season."

You never know. We never got to show our slides or explain what we did to the minister. Nothing but small talk.

Whatever was communicated, we kept smiling at each other, bowing at the beginning and end. Clearly, Donald was very happy and thought that this had been a very important moment. Jin-Ae was ecstatic; she couldn't wait to tell me how it was her who had found Donald, and by extension her who had achieved ministerial introduction for me, and that she had always known how important Donald was, how amazing our business together would be, and so on and so on – and basically that I could not function without her.

I suspected I humoured her too much.

By the end of the following day, I knew it for sure.

WEEK 1 - DAY 6
SATURDAY SIGHTSEEING AND STRIFE IN SHANGHAI

Saturday was a day with no meetings and no travel, dedicated to exploring the city. We'd seen a lot from a distance from just being driven around the city all week, but this was an opportunity to walk and take it at my own pace. Or, rather, since I could hardly leave her behind, at Jin-Ae's pace.

We left the hotel calmly, both of us (I thought) in a good mood. It didn't take long, though, for her to launch into a harangue. I'm sure she'd been rehearsing.

Which is how I found myself being interrogated while she dragged me on repeat circuits around the square outside the Oriental Pearl Tower. Well, of course, she didn't have me on a lead and physically pull me along behind her, but by the second or third circuit it felt that way. We had been walking towards the tower, with the intention of being good tourists and going right to the top for the view, when suddenly, without prelude, and sounding uncharacteristically loud and aggressive, she started questioning me. Or, rather, interrogating. To my ear, I find Chinese people often have a hard and relatively high-pitched voice anyway, and Jin-Ae's had gone an octave above her standard delivery. To squeeze a word in edgeways, I found myself needing to shout. It wasn't turning into an argument – yet – but it wouldn't have been good to go into the lobby or any public areas with this exchange going on, so we walked round and round the square outside, the conversation getting more and more heated with each circuit we completed.

What was that all about? It wasn't that something terrible had happened. I'd not done anything wrong in the previous week, or at least nothing she wanted to complain about. Following logic known only to her, she'd decided that this was the right time to ask about her salary, or rather, how much I was going to raise it by. And, while most other people I'd known to ask me for pay rises went about that topic in a deferential or gently pleading way, Jin-Ae's approach was simply to demand – that I give her what she considered to be her rightful remuneration.

In retrospect, what I should have done was to say that it wasn't my decision, and we would have to discuss it with HR and the other directors when we got back to London, and tell her that was the necessary protocol. However, right then we didn't have anyone solely dedicated to HR, let alone much in the way of formal procedures, and she knew it. Because she thought of me as the boss, she assumed I could make any decision I wanted. The only one I was prepared to make right then, though, was to be sure that we did form a remuneration committee as soon as I got back to the office.

I should have seen this coming, I really should. I had spent enough time with her by now to work out her modus operandi, but I hadn't expected her to raise the subject here, and just one week into a three-week trip. Naturally, I tried saying simply that we'd discuss it back in London, but she wouldn't let it lie. Worse, rather than simply talking about how much she should be paid – she hadn't put a number on it yet, but it was easy to foresee that when she did, her demand would be unrealistic – she wanted to ask and discuss how much everyone else in the London office was earning. More accurately, all the other women; I think she assumed (wrongly, at least in the case of our company) that men always earned more and therefore weren't a valid comparison. If one wanted proof of the adage that women are critical of other women, Jin-Ae was offering up a masterclass.

"How much does Greta earn?" she queried.

"I can't tell you," I replied.

"I bet it is more than £30,000 – is it?"

"I can't tell you."

"Greta is useless, she does nothing. I am worth three or four Gretas."

"Greta does a lot, and she has been with us for a long time. She is not even in the same office as you, so you cannot know how much she does."

"So, you are admitting that she earns more than £30,000?!"

"No, I'm not. I don't remember the amount, and even if I did, I wouldn't tell you."

"I don't believe you, you know all the numbers."

And so on, and so on, switching focus from Greta to Hannah to Susan. The haranguing went on and on, and I couldn't help getting worked up; by now, even if I had known the numbers, I wouldn't have been able to remember them as I'd stopped remembering anything. My brain was turning to porridge. We were walking round and around a 500-metre-high tower that looked rather like two globes with a skewer through them, not so much arguing about Jin-Ae's salary expectations as having her assassinate the character, competence and pay of all her colleagues, and forcing me to defend them. I would happily have done so, but not there and then, and not in response to her demands. This was more than surreal – it was infuriating.

Eventually it stopped. I don't know who gave up first, but we must have made some sort of truce, as we continued our sightseeing for the rest of the day without further argument. Any hope I might have had that this had put the lid on things, and that she would not raise the subject again until we got back to London, however, was utterly misplaced.

My refusal to engage with her salary demands meant I'd obviously dropped further in Jin-Ae's estimation, not that it would have been a long fall now that her opinions of me had become more obvious. She did nothing to go up in mine over the next few hours. Even leaving aside the argument we'd just had, I now discovered that although she'd claimed that she knew all the important places to go in the city, she obviously didn't. She'd implied, though not actually said, that she had been to Shanghai before, and knew it quite well. Obviously not. My guess was that she'd tried to memorise an out-of-date guidebook. We got lost. Several times. She could simply have said that the city was changing so fast that her knowledge was out of date, which would have made sense. However, that would have been admitting that she wasn't perfect, and after our morning argument, today of all days was not one when she was going to do that.

Whilst I could easily have understood and accepted that it was difficult to find a particular temple because new tower blocks had been built all around it (true; it was still there, but the entrance to the garden it was set in had been moved to a different street) it was a stretch to accept that we'd walked more than half a mile in the wrong direction down the river bank looking for the Bund, the old city centre. Neither it, nor the river, had moved.

Never mind; we walked. And we walked. Many more miles than necessary, but apart from getting more exercise, that meant we saw also bits of Shanghai that most tourists don't, some of them memorable. It's rare that I think back to random meanderings around a new city as having been a waste of time, and certainly this was not one of those occasions. We viewed those hyper-modern office blocks up close, and wondered where all the businesses to occupy them came from, or if they were largely empty; if the Chinese had built them in the expectation of future world domination. Difficult to judge on a Saturday afternoon. At ground level, we saw the new shops, the designer boutiques, all glass and marble, but almost all of them devoid of people, apart from smartly suited staff, all trying to look busy, but with no customers at all to attend to. We joined a large crowd watching a fashion parade on a stage constructed on the pavement outside a department store, then went inside and found ourselves to be the only customers.

Then, getting lost again, we stumbled upon a piece of old Shanghai, narrow streets with semi-derelict houses, the antithesis of modern, where foreigners are probably not expected to go ever; the locals, though, were there in strength. We wandered into a market hall and almost got crushed. Plenty of customers here. Just none, other than a few window shoppers, in the designer shops in the modern city centre.

We'd walked miles and we'd had a debilitating argument; exhausting and emotionally draining. Now, I was hungry. There were plenty of places around where we could have eaten, but Jin-Ae insisted that we go to a street food market. Before this trip to Shanghai, I hadn't heard about them, but I've been to many since. They usually open in the late afternoon or early evening, and there are brightly lit stalls, all jostling for space, selling every kind of street food you can think of and plenty that you can't, including, famously, the things that most of us can't imagine ever wanting to eat, like locusts and scorpions and snails and all kinds of creepy-crawlies, all skewered and fried or barbecued.

Jin-Ae asked directions from someone, who pointed the way to a street market nearby. On the way there, Jin-Ae told me how good street food hygiene was in China, how every stall was inspected, everything checked every day, and so on. Quite reassuring and, given the control-freakery of the Chinese, perfectly credible.

I didn't then know that street food markets only open in the evening, but obviously Jin-Ae didn't either. It was mid-afternoon now. It didn't look like the street that we were in accommodated a food market at any hour of the day or night.

It did, however, have one solitary food stall, and that was open. Other than this, the street, which looked more residential than business, was quiet; no people around besides us and the stall holder. His speciality – well, his only offering – was fried dumplings. Fine by me. By the time we got there I'd happily have eaten scorpions or snails or anything at all. I didn't think the dumplings tasted very good – having spent a few days in Shanghai, I was now a more discerning diner – but I was too hungry to care.

I told Jin-Ae I didn't want to walk back to the centre, but we were now quite a way from it and this wasn't a place where we'd be likely to find a taxi. The stall holder pointed us to a nearby bus stop. Shanghai buses weren't very modern in those days, or at least the one we caught wasn't; there was standing room only, and a hundred other swaying bodies crushed against us. I thought it was fun – I always enjoy going by regular bus in cities I'm visiting for the first time – but Jin-Ae clearly didn't. She tugged at my arm and got off at the very next stop. My immediate assumption was that she'd decided buses weren't her style, but it wasn't that – much to her shame and embarrassment, she was violently sick in the gutter. Perhaps the dumplings weren't up to the usual hygiene standards she'd been telling me about, and that's why they hadn't tasted so good. Maybe she had found the day too emotional also. Whatever the cause, and fortunately for me, I wasn't stricken the same way.

When she felt a bit better, we got lucky with a passing cab, so could get back to the hotel in comfort. She raced off to her room. On my own at last. Luxury! Now I could relax in the lounge, drink as much wine as I liked, savour some high-quality dumplings and later, replete, fall into bed.

WEEK 2 - DAY 0
SUNDAY – OFF TO SEOUL

Sunday was a travel day, headed to another destination new to me – Seoul, capital of South Korea. I was going to meet some of our existing customers there – local subsidiaries of our international customers – but our prime business goal was to try to sell our international services to new customers.

Whilst it had been obvious from the start that trying to sell to Chinese companies would be a completely unrealistic challenge, at least until such time as we had a Chinese operation, Korea was a different matter. Big business in China, such as it was, was government controlled or influenced, whilst Korea was a free and very capitalist market. Also, whilst China was the logical place to look at setting up a regional back-office operation, we knew in advance that wouldn't be economic in Korea, where costs were high. We'd also figured that whilst both Korean and Japanese companies would probably agree to deal with a

Chinese operation, even if they had to hold their noses from time to time, Korean companies wouldn't willingly deal with the Japanese or vice versa.

But first we had to get to the airport in Shanghai, which presented an opportunity to experience the super-fast Maglev (magnetic levitation) train that had started operating just a couple of years earlier. It's still the fastest train in the world, reaching 431km/h, taking passengers right into the airport in just over seven minutes. To do the same journey by road would take at least thirty. It's not as popular as you'd expect. The problem is that the terminus station isn't anywhere near the centre of Shanghai. It's not even an attractive area with hotels and restaurants and shops. Other than the station, it all looks a bit run down. Now there are subway lines that connect to the station, but back then, the only way to get there was by taxi – and the journey from our hotel, even on a Sunday morning with little traffic around, took nearly half an hour. We could probably have made it all the way to the airport in the same time, but I was determined to try the train.

Somewhat disappointingly, there's nothing special about the train itself, just modern carriages with aircraft-type seating. There's not even any interesting scenery along the way. The highlight of the journey is focusing on the illuminated speed display at the end of each carriage, watching it rise gradually from zero to around 350, and then suddenly spurt up to the maximum 431 before the train decelerates and coasts into the airport station. The highest speed is only maintained for about half a minute. You don't travel this way because it's an efficient way to get to the airport. You do it for the experience. But, small boy at heart that I am, I've still done it again when visiting Shanghai more recently.

Our flight from Shanghai to Seoul was with China Eastern, and was the first time I had flown with a Chinese airline. The plane was modern enough, the same sort of Airbus or Boeing that any Western airline flies, although with truly ghastly pale green upholstery. The most remarkable difference was that nobody seemed to care about inflight safety. The usual announcement about turning off mobile phones was largely ignored; nearby passengers just continued their conversations throughout take-off, stopping only when they lost signal; the passenger across the aisle from me looked at his phone as if it had done him a personal injury. Another got up and tried to walk to the bathroom while the plane was still climbing steeply; that was actually quite hilarious and would have made a great Chinese-style Mr Bean video clip.

I've been to hundreds of airports around the world. As a rule, only the bad ones leave an impression on me. Seoul's airport, Incheon, delivered quite the opposite reaction. It's wonderful – at least as airports go. Nice building, efficient processes, a pleasure to arrive at, surely a contender for World's Best Airport. The rest of Seoul doesn't live up to the promise of its airport, but it gives a great first impression. Perhaps you think I'm weird, but there are lots of business travellers like me; if you've got to use airports, best to take an interest in them, right?

It's a long way from Incheon airport to downtown Seoul, 50km, a much longer journey than between airport and city in Shanghai. However, whilst in Shanghai it's mostly across flat and empty agricultural land, almost all the drive into

Seoul is through built-up suburbs. It was twilight, so not a good time to judge, but a lot of it looked quite run down. Certainly, dowdy by comparison with modern Shanghai. Our hotel, however, stood out; a modern tower, covered completely with gold coloured mirror glass, approached by a long sweeping ramp, just the right image to ensure that Jin-Ae immediately approved. Perhaps she didn't notice that the hotel was built on top of a bus station.

Following the routine we'd established, we met up in the hotel lounge to review the schedule for the coming week. In Korea, almost every business seems either to be part of, or associated with, the "chaebols". These are family-owned and controlled conglomerates with deep and mysterious government influence – it's never been clear to me whether the government controls the chaebols or the chaebols control the government; I suspect the latter. There are several dozen of them, but five really huge ones that are known worldwide, each amongst the world leaders in their own sectors.

I was impressed that Jin-Ae had lined up meetings with three of the biggest – Hyundai, Samsung and LG. She'd dedicated a day to each; the meeting was only likely to be one hour in each case, max, but this time we were the sales team rather than the customers, so good preparation was critical. The type of service we sold involved processing and managing energy and environmental data for all the individual premises that a company owned or operated, whether manufacturing site, warehouse, office, shop or anything else. Big multinationals often operate thousands of sites around the world; even where they practice centralised management, it's extremely unlikely that they have any single employee, or even a dedicated department, that knows about all of them. The executives that we were likely to meet this week certainly wouldn't know the detail, but it was wise to assume that they'd have a good grasp of the high-level numbers – and the potential savings our services might offer to them.

What made it more complicated than with western companies, but arguably a better business opportunity for us, was that Korean chaebols are perhaps the only true conglomerates left on earth. Samsung, the biggest, not only makes the ubiquitous mobile phones, TVs and white goods known around the world, but cars and heavy machinery too, mainly sold in Asia. They also own a bank, insurance company and shops, and their property portfolio in Korea extends to many residential buildings. I knew some of this, but not a great deal. Jin-Ae told me that more detailed information was hard to come by on the internet, even in Korean language.

I'd learnt over the years that to be successful in selling services to multinationals, it helps to know more about the company, or at least the points relevant to your business, than the person you're selling them to. It helps to surprise them with facts and figures that they feel they ought to know; you don't want to embarrass them, and make them reveal their surprise, but you do want them to be impressed that you've done your research.

That meant we needed to get the best information we could about every company we would visit and prepare an individual presentation for each; just as importantly, I needed to immerse myself in that presentation beforehand, so that I could put on the best possible show. The risk for me that I could foresee happening here in Korea, but had never had to consider before with any potential client in other countries, was that I might mix up what the companies did. So, like everyone else in the West, I knew that Samsung made electronics and Hyundai made cars; however, Samsung also makes cars, and Hyundai also has an electronics division. And both of them have their fingers in a myriad of other pies too. When presenting to Hyundai, I needed to think Hyundai, and when presenting to Samsung, think Samsung. I put my brain on alert.

And all that before considering that I'd never tried to sell services in Korea or any other country in Asia before, and that these were three of the world's largest companies – potential clients to die for.

Hence the reason for dedicating one day to each of the three companies. Or the equivalent thereof. The meetings were all scheduled in the late morning. The plan was that we would review and rehearse the presentation immediately after breakfast, before going to the morning meeting; then, after it was over and we'd had lunch, prepare the next company's presentation for the following morning.

Those meetings were on Wednesday, Thursday and Friday. First, we had some other business. Our American car manufacturing customer had a plant near Seoul, and I was going there on Monday to do a site visit and review, just as I had done on my trip round South America a few years earlier.

WEEK 2 - DAY 1
MONDAY – KOREAN BUSINESS CULTURE

I left Jin-Ae in the hotel making calls and working on some remaining bits of research that she hadn't been able to do from London, and that she thought would be important for the meetings later in the week. She didn't seem very happy that I was going off on my own to the car factory. I don't know if she was feeling left out of a different and possibly entertaining day, or if she thought that I wouldn't be able to do the visit without her assistance, even if only as a translator and critic. I frankly didn't care what she was thinking any more; I was quite happy to have a day to get out and do something straightforward that I'd previously done in thirty or forty other factories around the world. As you'll have gathered from the South American tour in Part One of this book, every one of the plants is different, but I followed the same routine in all of them. I also thought an outing like that would help me learn a little about how business is done in Korea, as that could be useful for the sales meetings. I believe it did; I certainly got some interesting insights into the culture!

The taxi ride to the plant was a long one. This time in daylight, so I could see that suburban Seoul has as varied a mix of new and old buildings, rich and poor neighbourhoods, as London or most other long-established cities. So different to Shanghai, where they'd either demolished or hidden anything old and shabby.

I was met at the gatehouse by a very exuberant young man, who introduced himself as Song-Jun. He seemed genuinely excited to see me. Excessively so. I assume it was because he'd been given the 'honour' of meeting an Englishman and so had an opportunity to practice his English with a native. Not that he hung around chatting; he walked fast, and I got out of breath just keeping up, and it seemed like a mile to the office building he was taking me to. Song-Jun didn't stop talking all the way, pointing at this building and that, and telling me the purpose of each. He'd missed his vocation as a tour guide. He's the first – and still the only – person I've ever met who could talk animatedly and enthusiastically for several minutes about a generator house (something essentially identical to a small concrete garage with grilles at the end). And you should have heard him wax lyrical about the shed where they kept the forklift trucks!

We finally reached the office, and I was ushered into a meeting room, collecting tea on the way. Out of a machine this time. Very corporate. Song-Jun was very excited that his bosses wanted to meet me, and went off to find them. A few minutes of peace and quiet to get my breath back! The walk from the gatehouse to the office had only taken about fifteen minutes, but at the speed we walked, and with Song-Jun's non-stop running commentary, it felt like it had taken hours.

It was a deflated Song-Jun that returned ten minutes later. His bosses were all busy now, so couldn't come to meet me; that was no problem for me, but he clearly thought that it was some sort of personal failure on his part.

To refocus and re-energise him, I showed him a short presentation to explain what I was hoping to achieve on my visit; I'd given it dozens of times before. Finished, I shut the laptop, and suggested we continue the plant tour, thinking we'd better do that while I still had some energy left.

We stood up, but before we could leave, the door was opened by a slightly older man, perhaps early 30s, and Song-Jun introduced him as his immediate boss. We sat down again. I found myself exchanging some small talk; he did speak and understand English, but nothing like as well as Song-Jun. It took some minutes, and an awkward silence, for me to realise that the younger man had not spoken one word since introducing his boss. Silently, he pointed at the laptop. An unspoken hint that I should show the presentation again. No problem.

I'd hardly finished doing that re-run when the door opened again, and a much older man appeared. He was probably only in his fifties, but he was the oldest Korean that I met on that trip. He introduced himself; "I am the Engineering Director." So, Song-Jun's boss's boss. I think that was the limit of his spoken English.

The middle manager pointed to the laptop – now *he* had gone silent on me! I gave the presentation for a third time. The director kept nodding and smiling. I was pretty sure he didn't understand a word I was saying, but perhaps he could read the words on the screen. No way of knowing. Just as well there were only a few slides; it's dispiriting giving a presentation to someone who appears to neither understand nor care.

When I finished, the senior turned to the middle manager and spoke to him in Korean. He, in turn, first told me to "wait please" and turned to speak to his junior. Song-Jun now spoke to me in English.

"Mr Park wants to know why you are here."

Great, so much for having given an explanation three times. I decided to keep it simple.

"I've come to visit the factory and collect some information from Song-Jun that we need for the Head Office project."

Song-Jun dutifully translated, addressing himself to his boss, who in turn then spoke to his. A surreal experience of Asian attitudes to seniority and age. In this place, if there was someone more senior than you in the room, you couldn't or wouldn't say a word unless asked. Speak only when you're spoken to! Was this the norm in Korea?

My answer was obviously adequate, and clearly everyone considered the meeting finished. The bosses stood up, we bowed to each other, as one does, and they left the room in the reverse order to their arrival, separately, opening the door and shutting it behind them each time. Duty done.

My first lesson in Korean business culture. It left me wondering how people got promoted; Song-Jun was obviously very smart and capable, but if he could only do what he was told to do, and only speak when spoken to, was he ever given an opportunity to show initiative for which he could be rewarded? Or did he just have to wait until the most senior boss retired, and then he and his immediate boss would all move up a rung? Is this how it used to be everywhere? Maybe even here in England companies exist where something like this still goes on. Come to think of it, it must work a bit like that in some branches of the public sector.

WEEK 2 - DAY 2
TUESDAY – MORE LESSONS IN KOREAN BUSINESS CULTURE

The next day, Tuesday, brought another strange and interesting lesson. Back in Shanghai, we'd established that the Chinese could manage both data processing and customer service calls in Japanese but, although they had people who could read and translate written Korean, it would be difficult to get staff who could speak the language to an adequate standard and who were prepared to work on relatively routine activities for low salaries. That meant that we would need some support in Korea itself. Jin-Ae had found just one company that she thought we could work with, and we went to see them in downtown Seoul on the Tuesday morning.

I thought the meeting went well. I'm always happy to come across all-female management teams and, from what I was told, those are even more unusual in Korea than in the UK or USA. The person there who impressed me most was Yoonah; she spoke near-perfect English, was very professional, and told us of her many years of experience. Had she been in Shanghai, she'd have been nearly old enough to lead the team at Great Wall! Jin-Ae remained silent throughout the meeting, though; either she'd got the message about age respect and only speaking when spoken to or, more likely I suspected at that time, she was pissed off that she wasn't needed to translate anything.

Once our business was done, Yoonah suggested we might like to stay for another hour and help her with some final interviews for new staff, the next thing in her diary. I'm glad I did, as it revealed another aspect of Korean business culture I could never have expected.

These were young people interviewing for a similar job to the one we'd want them to do, a customer service representative, but for another company. The successful candidate was going to be communicating mainly in English, so the interview would also be in English. They'd had some initial interviews and whittled down a shortlist to four finalists.

I hadn't ever thought of interview candidates as 'finalists', but there's no better word for how this was handled. It was literally a knock-out competition. Jin-Ae and I sat next to Yoonah, at one end of a fairly long table. Two of the finalists came in together and sat at the other end, one on each side. Yoonah first asked each of them, "Why would you be good at this job?" and gave them a few minutes to answer. Nothing unusual there. But then, the killer question.

"Why would you be better at this job than the other candidate sitting opposite you?"

Two minutes to respond to that. I don't know whether the candidates had ever met each other, but if any of them had been friends before, they certainly wouldn't have been after this trial! It was even more brutal than it sounds; instant character assassination of someone else just like them, sitting only a metre away.

The duel over, the two candidates were told to leave. Yoonah told us which of the two she liked best, and asked if I agreed, which, as it happens, I did.

We had a similar exercise with the other two finalists. Then, the 'winner' of each of the two sessions went head-to-head, with different questions; Yoonah presented them with a hypothetical situation and asked them both how they would handle it – and then asked each of them to critique the other. Finally, Yoonah picked the one she liked best, in front of the other one.

"You're hired," to one of them, "You're fired," to the other.

Just imagine; it would surely never be allowed in Europe or America (except, perhaps, on TV in *The Apprentice*). It would be a nerve-wracking experience for a professional sales person, but it must be shocking for a twenty-something-year-old, looking for their first job. And in this case, just an entry level customer service role; not one with important management responsibilities. Imagine getting rejected, and then going elsewhere, and having to go through it all again – and then again, and again. Next time you talk to someone in a call centre, try to guess how well the person would have done in a test like that, and whether they'd ever have got employed had they been in Korea.

But that wasn't the only interesting thing I learned that morning.

There were both male and female finalists, but while the women looked to be in their early 20s, the men were clearly much older, around 30. All of them after the same job. Coincidence? Apparently not. Korea still has compulsory military service for men, with one of the longest service periods in the world: about two years. As soon as young men graduate from university, they're sent to do military service – from what I saw on later visits, that mostly means parading back and forth along the border with North Korea, trying to look as scary as a scared young man can manage. After that, those that come from better-off families are sent abroad to study English or do Masters' degrees, so they're already at least 27 or 28 years old by the time they're ready to join the employment queue. Girls, on the other hand, don't do military service, or get sent abroad by their parents, who expect them to go straight into work from university, so are in their very early twenties when they start to look for jobs. I hope that equality has improved in the last fifteen years since my trip! However, I was pleased to note that in the final duel, the 22-year-old woman got the job, beating a 29-year-old man.

One finalist, explaining why they'd be better than the person opposite them, said that as she lived within walking distance and had no commitments, she would put in longer hours. After she'd gone (and been rejected) I asked Yoonah why someone looking for this type of job would think that working long hours would be an advantage. "Everyone works long hours here," she told me. Korean business culture apparently requires employees to get into the office in the morning before their boss does, and only leave after the boss has gone home. She told me it's quite usual for office workers, even those doing relatively routine (what we would consider nine-to-five) jobs, to work from 7 in the morning to 9 or 10 at night, every day.

Back in the hotel on Tuesday afternoon, Jin-Ae and I got down to the business of adapting and honing the presentation I would give to Hyundai, our first Korean sales meeting, the next day. I would present in English, with English language slides; Jin-Ae was going to produce a translated version and give the attendees memory sticks on which there would be both English and Korean versions. We'd worked on the basic presentation in London, and I was happy with it. However, Jin-Ae wasn't; she had a perfectionist streak that I lack, at least when it comes to presentation slides. I do insist that the spelling and grammar are correct, but I can't get overly fussed about minor graphical details. After all, each slide is only up on screen for a few moments. Nevertheless, I can't criticise someone who wants to get everything exactly right. A second opinion, however much I may be irritated by it, is always welcome.

We changed words here and there, moved the order of slides around a bit, made fonts bigger and smaller, moved images a few millimetres left, right, up and down, and time moved on. A lot. We'd reached a point where we were making changes for change's sake. I was now having difficulty keeping my cool, and I wanted a drink and dinner. It was well past 8pm, and we'd now spent six hours editing a presentation that would take about 40 minutes to deliver. The thought occurred to me that Jin-Ae may have taken to heart the earlier lesson about staff never finishing work until their bosses had left. Seemed like a good idea to test the theory. With a show of great resignation, she agreed to stop, reluctantly admitting that it was "almost good enough".

WEEK 2 - DAY 3

WEDNESDAY – THE FIRST KOREAN SALES PRESENTATION AND AN INTERESTING DINNER

I arrived for breakfast with Jin-Ae the next morning, determined to head off any potential arguments. Even before sinking my teeth into the first croissant, I told her I wanted no more changes to the presentation, and that I intended just to rehearse the last version from the previous night. If, after today's sales meeting, she felt that anything needed improving, or something had been misunderstood or was downright wrong, we'd review that together in the afternoon and make appropriate changes to the presentation for Thursday's meeting. Most of the slides would be the same, anyway.

"Sure, you're the boss."

I was a little unnerved by that compliant response. Was I now engaged in a game of triple-bluff. Perhaps really she was thinking, "But not much longer, if I have anything to do with it…"

The taxi journey to Hyundai wasn't as uneventful as I'd expected. I was about to 'enjoy' an entirely new experience. For the first time, Jin-Ae decided to get close up and personal, and I didn't like it one bit. We were side by side on the back seat, as per usual. Suddenly, without warning, she turned towards me and, whilst holding her body as far away from me as the confines of the taxi allowed, stretched out her arm towards me and began flicking at the shoulders of my jacket with her long carmine-red fingernails.

"You have dandruff."

I didn't think I did, and I couldn't see any white specks. She seemed to be flicking for the sheer hell of flicking; I decided to grimace and bear it. One can't see much of one's own shoulders, and no doubt her eyesight was sharper than mine. I couldn't imagine any fall was significant anyway – us bald men don't have much hair, so surely not much risk of dandruff, and I'd washed what little I had in the shower before leaving. But, after my initial surprise, what she was doing seemed more amusing than intrusive, and I certainly preferred her to care what I looked like rather than let me go in looking a mess.

Tactic two, though, was definitely intrusive, and came as a very unpleasant shock. I later called it the 'Reverse Chameleon'. Instead of asking me to stick out my tongue, she was sticking her finger into my mouth and onto my tongue. It was the first and only personal skin contact we'd had, and not one I could imagine anyone enjoying. It took repetitions over several days (as she did this every day after this) for me to work out how and when she attacked – 'attack' being the *mot juste*. Not that I ever figured out a defence.

Her technique was to ask me something, anything, to make sure I was talking, and then interrupt, just as I had my mouth open. At that instant, she would push her finger into my mouth, putting a breath freshener on my tongue. She did that at lightning speed and before I could bite her finger off. Every time. Don't think I wouldn't have bitten that finger if she'd given me a chance!

I'd brushed my teeth, and hadn't thought I had bad breath, though I had no-one intimate around to confirm that. She seemed to agree I didn't smell foul or toxic. "Just in case," she said. I wasn't going to make a scene in the taxi, but she could see I wasn't happy; nevertheless, she repeated this every day, every remaining taxi journey we shared for the rest of our trip. Maybe for her it was another opportunity for evil domination, to put me in my place. She certainly wouldn't allow me to put the breath freshener – an inch-square jelly film, which tasted revolting – on my own tongue; don't imagine reading this that I didn't suggest it – repeatedly.

We got to Hyundai early, and the assistant who met us ushered us into a conference room to get set up. It was just as well that we had some time to get ready, as we were faced with the rigmarole of getting the presentation up on screen. In 2006, whilst almost every company's meeting rooms had data projectors, there was no uniformity. The world over, not just in Korea. First, if there wasn't a projector already in the room, you had to try to find someone to find someone else who knew where one was, and bring it. It never mattered if you'd told them in advance that you'd need one; wherever one went, the same drama played out. Most projectors were still as big and heavy as a microwave.

Once you had a projector, the next job was to connect the laptop to it. From experience, I travelled with a variety of cables, but still sometimes none of them fitted. From the viewpoint of the travelling business person, I'd hazard that the single most helpful technical development of the last decade must have been the USB connector. But not always. And not then.

Finally, the screen resolution had to be sorted. For those readers who don't have a clue what I mean here, the 'resolution' is the number of dots (technically pixels) per inch of the screen. The more dots, the clearer the picture. Every new technological development seems to bring with it higher resolutions, which means more dots (sorry pixels) per inch, and clearer pictures.

If the resolution of the projector wasn't compatible with the laptop, the picture would either be too small or part of it would disappear, and sometimes text was illegible. Sometimes the projector only supported 640x480 resolution, that of the first colour screens; when that happened it was very bad news, because if the presentation had any graphics or unusual fonts, it was guaranteed to look awful.

Apart from being time consuming, setting up a presentation is one of those things that's always stressful at a time when one wants to be cool, calm and collected. When the attendees are already in the room, that just makes the stress worse. Nevertheless, sometimes, depending on the audience, it can be turned into an entertainment. It can even be a bonding experience; I once made a long-lasting friendship with the CEO of a well-known multinational when we both got down on our hands and knees under a conference room table, spending twenty minutes trying to work out which cable connected to what.

Fortunately, this time I was connected and ready just in time, albeit with only a few seconds to spare. Time to welcome the audience. Jin-Ae had told me to expect just two people, the engineering manager and his assistant, but, exactly on the hour, nearly twenty people filed into the room. There weren't enough chairs, so the last ones to come into the room had to stand. Never mind; they were obviously expecting this eventuality, and they were clearly the juniors anyway – the body language fitted with what I'd found on my first day in Seoul.

Having an unexpectedly big audience didn't faze me; I'd learnt long ago, early in my business life, that you might expect an audience of one and get a hundred, or expect a hundred and just get one. It seemed to upset Jin-Ae momentarily, though, as I could see her surreptitiously counting under the table how many memory sticks she'd prepared.

I've always been a confident presenter, but this time was different. I was apprehensive. It wasn't the audience or the venue, or that anyone would be offended by my beard, but more that it was my first sales meeting in Asia. Jin-Ae had wound me up about the need to adapt to the culture, and that had hit home in some aspects. Looking out at the room full of enthused Korean businessmen, old and young, I began to doubt, however, that she had understood the nuances of this culture herself. These people didn't look anything like as serious as I'd expected. In fact, the assembled company looked more like a class of students fronted by a couple of elderly, but smiling and indulgent, teachers. But still I was uneasy. With what I'd learnt of Korean business culture over the previous two days, I worried I might say the wrong thing or make some inappropriate gesture, something that was innocent back home but might be construed differently here.

Nonetheless, the presentation seemed to go well. Nods and smiles from the elders, furious scribbling in notepads by the younger contingent. There were a lot of questions afterwards, which should have been great; unfortunately, though, all of them seemed to relate to our existing car manufacturing client. They'd obviously hoped I'd be a rich source of trade secrets, and kept pumping me for information. I don't think they asked a single thing about the services I was trying to sell them. In the presentation I'd only mentioned the name of the customer as one of a list of existing clients; I wondered why they thought I knew so much about that client. I suspected Jin-Ae had told them something when she'd been trying to arrange the meeting, but this wasn't something I could stop and ask her now.

So, it wasn't a very good Q&A session; either I didn't know the answer ("how many coats of paint do they put on this model of car?") or wouldn't tell even if I could remember ("how many litres of water and kilowatt-hours of electricity are consumed per vehicle?"). Anything which I know that relates to a customer is obviously confidential. I'm not sure my not answering mattered from their perspective – I got the impression that the younger and more junior ones were just trying to come up with important-sounding questions in order to impress their bosses.

But sessions like that always leave me thinking. If I don't answer, will they believe that I don't know, or maybe that I

241

think facts such as those aren't important? If I won't pass on any confidential information, and they can see that I never will, does that mean they'll never do business with us? Or does it reassure them? If I say something that I don't think is secret, but a member of the audience does, will that stop them from doing business with us because I might share information about them with another competitor in a future similar meeting? And the niggling and then growing thought that perhaps they only agreed to the meeting because they knew we provided services to a competitor and might be tempted to give away information, consciously or unconsciously.

For whatever reason, this visit never realised its objective of being the first introduction to selling our services. The senior people seemed very enthused afterwards and said what a useful meeting it had been; but then, in subsequent weeks, kept themselves unavailable from all attempts at follow-up. We never met again, and never sold them anything.

Back in the hotel, Jin-Ae and I spent a busy afternoon reviewing the morning meeting and preparing for the next day. 95% of the presentation was the same, but we made a lot of changes. Mostly these were at Jin-Ae's insistence, and pretty minor. Indeed, as far as I was concerned, they were irrelevant and unnecessary. But, as she kept telling me, she'd been "in the audience", so her perspective counted. True, but it didn't temper my irritation at moving an illustration from the left of the slide to the right, and then back to the left again, and experimenting over and again with different type sizes and fonts.

Thank goodness we couldn't go on all night, because we had a dinner date with Yoonah. When we'd met the day before, she'd been most concerned that we hadn't ever tried a Korean barbeque. She had been insistent that it was the best cuisine in the world; I doubted that, but was certainly looking forward to trying it for the first time. Even more so after four or five hours of editing slides with Jin-Ae!

It might be barbecue, but not as we know it. For a start, the Korean version isn't an outdoor meal. Where we went looked, on outward appearance, to be a very ordinary restaurant, but Yoonah, meeting us on the street, and perhaps guessing what I was thinking, was quick to assure us that, in her opinion, this was the best place in Seoul to try Korean BBQ. She'd brought a couple of colleagues with her, and they were equally enthusiastic.

I prefer unpretentious restaurants anyway and was actually quite glad it wasn't a posh white-tablecloth-and-cut-crystal-wineglass place. Mind you, it's highly unlikely there are any Korean BBQ restaurants with white tablecloths – if they didn't catch fire first, they'd certainly be filthy within minutes!

These kind of restaurants have mushroomed in cities around the world now, but for those who aren't familiar, diners sit round a table that has a big round hole – like a well – in the middle. Rather like Shanghai Hot Pot tables, but in place of boiling stock, the waiter drops a bucket of glowing charcoal into the well and puts a grille over it. Diners pick up pieces of meat or fish with their chopsticks, griddle them briefly over the embers, and then roll the cooked morsel with their selection of sauces in a lettuce leaf, rather as one constructs a Chinese duck roll, before munching.

And then there is kimchi. The condiment on every table. Always. Everything in Korea seems to be eaten with kimchi, even if, as is often the case, kimchi is one of the ingredients in the dish. It's basically cabbage pickled with red chilli powder, or flakes, and salt. Think chilli-infused sauerkraut, though the cabbage pieces are bigger. I'm told most recipes include dried salted seafood – shrimps or anchovies – but there are hundreds of variants. Almost every home cook in Korea makes their own, and every year, in November, there's the Kimchi Festival, a sort of street party, when thousands of them stand at tables outside their houses preparing their kimchi for the year ahead, exchanging recipes and sharing jars of their creations with households less fortunate than their own.

I didn't fall in love at first bite with Kimchi. I like almost all food, and certainly love trying new things, and I love pickles and spicy food. Kimchi tasted interesting, but that was it. But, in deference to my hosts, and being assured that every Korean eats kimchi every day and as a result lives to a great age, I savoured modest quantities with my lettuce-wrapped meat, and did my best to look enthusiastic as different varieties were pushed towards me. Sorry; they all tasted the same.

A Korean barbeque, like all cook-at-table restaurants, proved to be great fun.

Well, it was fun once I'd got the hang of Korean chopsticks. Not all chopsticks are created equal! Korean ones are different from Chinese or Japanese; they're very short, metal rather than wood or plastic, and with a flat cross-section, rather than being square or round. I was adept with Chinese chopsticks, but found these flat, short metal ones turned me into an even messier eater than I usually am. After a few more meals in Korea, I got a bit better, managing to hold on to them rather than dropping them all the time, but this was my first experience. Yoonah took pity on me and told me it was OK to eat the rolled-up lettuce leaf with my fingers. Given the mess I was making, I was very glad to be in friendly and uncritical company. Well, that was the Koreans. I didn't say that Jin-Ae wasn't critical, but it looked like she was having no more success than me.

Yoonah had been sympathetic to my chopstick problems – everyone had been quite happy laughing about it – but she wasn't so forgiving to Jin-Ae. I suppose that being Asian, she was assumed and expected to be an expert.

The conversation brought out some useful information that I might not otherwise have discovered.

I'd noticed earlier that the Koreans we'd met didn't always seem to understand Jin-Ae when she was speaking Korean. Now, one of Yoonah's colleagues asked Jin-Ae, in English, if she was North Korean. She'd never said anything to me about having any links to Korea; I'd always thought of her as Chinese. But now she told us that her parents had been born in what was now North Korea, and had moved to China to live when the war broke out, long before she was born; so, the Korean that Jin-Ae had learnt at her mother's knee was from the North – and, to my surprise, it was different to that spoken in the South. Different enough to be noticed.

Over the next few minutes, I learned that in South Korea, the language has changed a lot over the last fifty or so years and, by now, is quite altered from the language spoken in the North. As I understand it, the fundamental difference is that a lot of words derived from English have been added –

imagine the word spoken with a Korean accent and written down using phonetic characters. In fact, the written language is entirely phonetic, so if you know the sound associated with each letter, you can read aloud anything that's written. Or so I was told. Obviously, it must help to understand it too! Korean has a strict alphabet of just 24 phonetic characters, for which it thanks King Sejong the Great, who, nearly six hundred years ago in 1443, foresaw the arrival of the typewriter and computer keyboards. Well, maybe not exactly; but it remains a fact that the creation of the Han'jul alphabet led to Koreans having one of the earliest and highest literacy rates in the world. Their alphabet makes the written language much simpler than Chinese or Japanese, where characters are created by combining others.

Apart from the accent being different between North and South, the Northern (or original) language must sound very antiquated to a Southerner. It's much more than the difference between English and American; for us, it would be more the equivalent of hearing someone talk now in the English used by Shakespeare. No wonder that the people we had met had been raising their eyebrows or failing to understand Jin-Ae. Gadzooks… and hey nonny nonny!

Their questioning and implied criticism must have got to Jin-Ae. I noticed that after this over-dinner conversation she made a point of speaking English to Koreans whenever she could get away with it.

It wasn't just the talk about North Korea that embarrassed Jin-Ae; the conversation moved on to China. By then, we'd all had plenty of local beer and had moved on to shots of soju, a Korean distilled (so very alcoholic) rice wine. Suitably lubricated, Yoonah and her colleagues delighted in criticising and making fun of the Chinese, to the discomfort and irritation of Jin-Ae.

"You eat dogs in China."

"No, we don't."

"Oh yes, the Chinese eat anything with four legs! Well, except for tables."

Cue raucous laughter.

Some years later, I recounted this exchange to Donald in Shanghai. He was most upset, though far from insulted. He just thought that the joker had overlooked eating fish and insects.

"This is not true! Tell her the joke is wrong! We Chinese eat anything that moves – except for cars!" he said.

My new Korean friends didn't just have it in for the Chinese. Having been told our next stop was Tokyo, they moved on enthusiastically to a long litany of criticism of the Japanese. Despite the countries being separated by just 50km of water, I didn't find their prejudice surprising; it is widely known that the Koreans have never forgiven the Japanese for their occupation during the second world war, and these days they are fierce commercial enemies.

But after that they criticised the Americans, I suppose understandably as they have so many military personnel in Korea, and even the Australians, for no immediately obvious reason at all. Maybe it was only their innate politeness that stopped them criticising the British too; I have no doubt that to a different audience on another day they would have had plenty of things to say about we Brits, perhaps using me as a comic example.

Someone since has told me that the Koreans are the most prejudiced people on earth. Not a tag I think I'd choose to give to any nation; I haven't come across other examples, and cling to the hope that it was just a feature of that particular group with whom I shared company on that night.

WEEK 2 - DAYS 4 AND 5
THURSDAY AND FRIDAY – CONFIDENCE INCREASING

After the first one on Wednesday, the meetings on Thursday and Friday got progressively better. Whatever Jin-Ae thought, I don't believe it had anything to do with the colour or size of the text on the slides. I was no longer nervous, felt I was getting better at judging the mood of the audience and, as we didn't have any customers who were electronics manufacturers, I didn't get the sort of probing "industrial espionage" type of questions that I'd had at Hyundai. In fact, the Friday meeting went so well that I'd have been proud of my performance had the audience been British or American; but I probably misread my Korean audience, or maybe I was fooling myself, as nothing more came of it afterwards.

Others who have been successful in selling in Asia always stress that the key is persistence. More than anywhere else in the world, they say, it's essential to work first on building a relationship, which means keeping on going back; it might take a dozen or more meetings before getting the first sale. No doubt they're right. That's fine for companies that have a sales professional resident in the country; but in our case, our total global sales resource was just me and one other fellow director, both resident in the UK, and, however big the prize, there was no way we could justify going back to Seoul every month. We simply didn't have the time or resource. We struggled to follow up prospects that were just an hour's drive distant; these ones in Korea would have had to be really promising first time around to justify regularly making a twelve-hour flight and coping with an eight-hour time difference. We weren't the only ones; I'm convinced that the major reasons that markets such as Korea and Japan appear closed to foreigners are largely that selling takes a lot of repetitive effort and the countries are far away and expensive to travel to.

Perhaps, if I'd read (and believed) the business books before I went, and seriously thought about it, I'd have realised that we were unlikely ever to sell anything to a big Korean chaebol. I suppose I was foolish enough to think that we had such a wonderful product that they'd be wanting to strike a deal after the first meeting. I was also assuming Jin-Ae would do whatever follow up was necessary and useful. It wasn't to be. That said, I've never regretted the experience.

WEEK 2 - DAY 5
FRIDAY EVENING - EXPLORING SEOUL CITY CENTRE

By Friday afternoon, we'd finished our business for the week, and the weekend beckoned. An opportunity to explore Seoul! I was craving some time on my own; however, if I'd have told Jin-Ae that I wanted to go out solo, she would have seen it as a snub – I didn't feel that strongly about it, and I certainly didn't want to risk creating any new stress between us. We were two-thirds of the way through the trip, but with almost a whole week to go, with Japan and its important meetings coming up, I needed her on side. I didn't want to risk deliberately upsetting her.

First, a chance to try out the Seoul subway. So far, we'd been going everywhere by taxi, partly because most of our meetings had been outside the city centre, and partly to ensure that we arrived looking our best. Maybe, on public transport, Jin-Ae would have been too self-conscious to flick dandruff off my shoulders and push breath freshener into my open mouth, though I wouldn't have put money on it.

We headed towards the city centre. Looking at the map, it appeared fairly close to our hotel, but it was too far to walk. I wasn't sure how easy we'd find it to get around by subway; I was remembering my first visit to Tokyo in 2000, where navigating the trains had proved quite a challenge simply because of the lack of any signs in English. As I now discovered, there wasn't much English signage on the Seoul subway either, but more than I'd remembered in Japan, and helpfully they'd given every station a number, and it was easy to establish the methodology. Line 1 had stations 101 to 130, line 2 stations from 201 to 230, and so on. On the platform there were signs highlighting the station number you were currently at, with arrows on each side indicating whether the train was headed towards ascending or descending station numbers.

Even without that helpful feature, things like watching out for the right station name are easier in Korea than Japan, simply because the words are all short and there are such a limited number of characters in the alphabet. Recognise the number of characters in a name, and the shapes of the first and last ones, and it's relatively easy to spot what you're looking for. Not so in Japan, where there are many different symbols that, to an untrained Western eye, look very similar to each other. Back in 2000, it was difficult to find anyone who understood or spoke English, even in Tokyo, and near impossible – even in big hotels – in a provincial city like Gifu, where I'd gone to speak at a conference. I might still be wandering around that city today had I not worked out that the name of the railway station was written as five characters, the last one being a picture of a picnic table, and waited for a bus with that displayed on the front of it.

No such issue here in Seoul. I had the company of Jin-Ae, who could interpret for me. She took some delight in showing off by translating signs and posters, though I noticed that, presumably because of the comments made about her sounding North Korean, she was reluctant to open her mouth to locals except when English failed.

Unlike Japan six years earlier, though, Seoul was full of people who spoke English and were enthusiastic about practicing it. On that first subway journey – and then on every subsequent one I made in Seoul – some young person, seeing me sitting there, came over and asked if I was American, and if they could practice talking English with me. They always assumed I was American, I suppose because there are still lots of troops stationed in Korea; but then exclaimed with apparent joy when I told them I was British. Apparently we're an exotic race – in South Korea at least.

Similarly, in the street, one has only to stop to look at the map to be instantly surrounded by helpful locals wanting to point the way and, more importantly for them, practice their English. I'd not advise travellers to stop and check their maps in the streets of most big foreign cities, as sometimes it feels like one is begging to be mugged; Seoul, though, feels completely safe, and it's a real pleasure to meet with the locals and to be sure one will never get lost.

Seoul is a big, busy and affluent city, but not one with much visible ancient history. Massive destruction during the Korean War meant that the capital had to be relocated temporarily to another city. What ancient buildings remain have been restored; they've done it using modern materials, so that they look as pristine as if they were in Disneyland. And they're all overshadowed by modern skyscrapers.

In that sense, it was like Shanghai, but the atmosphere on the street was entirely different. The shops, instead of being sterile and largely empty showrooms, were packed with people buying things. Instead of hordes bustling past office towers but never entering (I never did work out where they were actually headed), workers here were going in and out of buildings in droves. So, whilst Shanghai on a Saturday resembled a state-of-the-art commercial city centre museum, with no-one in the shops and nothing to suggest that anyone was actually working in any of those 50-storey office towers, Seoul on a Friday afternoon was vibrant and alive.

We wandered the streets until nightfall. Personally, I'd then have gone back to the hotel, grabbed a glass of wine and a plate of noodles and squirreled myself away in my room for the rest of the evening. Jin-Ae had other ideas. She'd established that Seoul had the biggest evening retail market in Asia, an area called Dongdaemun, and that we absolutely had to go there.

I think she was expecting some sort of open-air market like the one we'd been to in Shanghai, just much bigger. This was very different. Although there were some street stalls, almost all the action was in multi-storey buildings. Some might call them malls, but that conveys an image of style and space. Think rather of older office buildings, repurposed, with floors partitioned into hundreds of small and rather basic shops, divided by relatively narrow (and therefore very crowded) walkways. Building after building, floor after floor. Easy to believe that there are 50,000 market stalls (even if each one looks more like a small shop), difficult to imagine how anyone would ever visit all of them in a single lifetime or, more to the point, find something they were actually looking for. Not that I imagine this worries the average Korean shopper; it seemed that a lot of the stalls/shops were selling exactly the same things, laid out exactly the same way, so I found moving from one floor of stalls to another becoming a Groundhog Day event. But the style, the sheer number of people, the noise. I like shops, I like markets, but this environment sped up retail fatigue like nowhere else I'd ever been to, before or since.

Jin-Ae wasn't happy about it either. Not for the same reasons, but because there weren't any bargains. Zero fake goods. Not even good cheap copies. And, when it came to clothing, whilst even market stalls in Shanghai had adopted the "less is more" philosophy – in that the items for sale were displayed for customers' admiration – the traders in this market had largely adopted the 'pile it high' approach, even if they weren't following through to the completion of the adage, 'sell it cheap'.

WEEK 2 - DAY 6
SATURDAY – SCREAMING IN SEOUL

On Saturday morning, we headed into the centre once again to continue our sightseeing. This time, our first stop was Gyeongbokgung Palace, the top tourist attraction. It was originally built in 1395, but restoration made it look almost new, at least at first sight. It is impressive.

The first hour or so of looking around the palace and museum went peacefully and pleasantly. The lull before the storm. That blew up just after we had stopped for refreshments, now walking towards the next tourist attraction on our itinerary. Any hopes I might have had that Jin-Ae had forgotten about the scene we'd created together the previous weekend in Shanghai, or the salary issue that had prompted it, or at least that she was going to hold off until we got back to London, were now shattered. Her opening lines, about how much everyone else got paid and why, whatever the amount, they didn't deserve it, came out as a replay of a recording from the week before.

That starter outburst was just the executive summary. Gaining volume and speed, she now went into expansive detail. It was not so much a storm as a tempest; there was no stopping her. She'd obviously prepared a detailed argument, rehearsed what she was going to say, and had decided that nobody, least of all me, was going to stop her. Perhaps it was inspired by all the presentations we'd worked on; if so, thank goodness she hadn't made PowerPoint slides, or had a data stick to present to me on closing. Person by person, she assassinated the character of every one of our colleagues in the London office, this time not sparing the males of the species.

At first, I stood in stunned silence, listening and trying to take in this tirade. Trying to understand how anyone could be so vitriolic about their colleagues. Trying to understand how anyone, however good they were, could seriously believe that they were so perfect. Or worth so much.

Finally, it reached a tipping point. I couldn't take it any longer.

Perhaps, during the previous weekend in Shanghai, I'd assumed that she was just venting and wasn't really serious.

Perhaps the weather in Shanghai had been better, and I had been in a more tolerant mood.

Perhaps she hadn't pushed her arguments quite so aggressively last time.

Perhaps all the "little touches" she liked to make, whether to presentation slides or my body, had finally got to me.

Whatever. I'd just had enough. I lost it. Lost it in a way that I don't think I ever have with anyone else, before or since. I am not proud of what happened, but it happened.

I think I screamed. She certainly did. I started to walk away, she followed. We continued to scream at each other. We were in the middle of a busy square. People stopped to look at us. A lot of people. I wonder now what they thought. That Jin-Ae was my wife? My lover? Surely not an ambitious employee haranguing her boss!

Reaching the street, I escaped. I saw a taxi and dived into it, headed for the hotel, room, shower… wash away the whole experience. An hour or two later, calmer, now craving a drink (no, honestly, I'm not an alcoholic), I made my way to the lounge.

A glass or two of wine later, she wandered up to my table. Cool too, as though nothing had happened between us.

"What time do we leave tomorrow?"

"10, after breakfast."

"OK. Good night." Saying which, she turned and left. Phew. But extraordinary. She perplexed me beyond reason.

I couldn't predict how the next few days would go, but knew that we needed to get through them with professionalism – and personal distance. She was proving impossible to be with, but I couldn't fault her work. She was dedicated, committed, hardworking, and had single-handedly organised good meetings that no-one else in our company could have managed. That included some excellent high-profile companies in Tokyo, and nothing would divert me from the mission now. This was a business trip, after all. It just didn't feel much like one any more.

I had to pray – a truly rare event for me – that she would not raise the subject of her salary again. I no longer entirely trusted myself to stay calm and reasoned if she tried it.

WEEK 3 - DAY 0
SUNDAY - OFF TO TOKYO

For the flight to Tokyo, I'd booked Asiana, another airline I hadn't flown before, and one of Korea's two major carriers. I was most impressed! Even though the flight was only around 90 minutes, we got served lunch, which was an opportunity to try another Korean speciality, Bibimbap. This is a bowl of cold rice topped with seasoned minced meat, various vegetables and an egg. I was surprised at first that the bowl seemed half-empty, until the attendant showed me that I had to mix everything up together, adding chilli sauce and soya sauce from tubes. Not because they'd found out that I was a messy eater; I imagine that almost anyone would struggle to keep everything in the bowl if it was filled to the rim. Anyway, it was delicious as well as entertaining; and, of course, it came with kimchi. Just to emphasise how dependent Koreans are on it, the attendants came round several times with extra helpings of kimchi (one was enough for me).

With such an interesting lunch, the flight went by in no time. We successfully navigated Narita airport and caught the express train to the city. We were staying in the centre of town and, after checking in at the hotel, went for a long walk through the shopping streets. Fortunately for me, Jin-Ae was now on her best behaviour, so I was content with her company.

None of the hotel chains for which I had loyalty points existed in Tokyo then, so no 'free' drinks or food. Better really; more opportunity to explore the city and its prandial delights.

First stop, therefore, a sushi restaurant; one of those exceptionally busy places where customers sit around a long oval-shaped bar, while the chefs stand in the centre preparing their delicacies, wrapping seaweed around rice or rice around seaweed, slicing raw fish, putting each pair of morsels on a different coloured plate, and loading them, as fast as they make them, to a conveyor belt that goes round the bar, in-between them and the customers. Diners pick plates from the conveyor at a speed that matches that of the chefs adding new ones. When sated, a waiter counts the plates of each colour, each representing a different price, and tots up the total. Nowadays there are plenty of such restaurants around the world, but not then; I'd first experienced one on my earlier visit to Tokyo and had been missing eating sushi ever since.

Jin-Ae assumed I had never been in a sushi bar before and insisted on explaining the system to me. I listened patiently; no more arguments, please! Although she had told me that she'd worked for a Japanese company back in China when she was younger, her explanation led me to doubt that she had actually ever been in one of these restaurants herself before. When it reached a point where she explained that the green powder in a pot by the side of each dining position was wasabi (Japanese green horseradish) and dipped her piece of sushi in it, my doubts were confirmed.

"That's actually powdered green tea."

"No, it's wasabi!" she insisted.

"Wasabi doesn't come as a powder."

"Oh yes it does."

At which point, the risk of getting involved in a pantomime exchange was defused by a waiter arriving with small dishes of wasabi paste…

WEEK 3 - DAY 1
MONDAY – MY FIRST PRESENTATION IN JAPAN

Jin-Ae arrived for breakfast in a foul mood, complaining about the hotel. The fact that we didn't qualify for their lounge, so had to go to the regular restaurant with all the *hoi polloi*, was a minor inconvenience to her compared to the big issue of the day.

"This is not a good hotel. There was no toothbrush in my room. I asked reception, and they told me I had to go to the shop and buy one."

"Most of the hotels I've stayed in don't put complimentary toothbrushes in the room," I told her.

"You must stay in bad hotels, then. All the hotels I have stayed in give toothbrushes."

I wondered how many, if any, hotels she'd stayed in before this trip. If, like her, you judge hotels on their provision of toiletries, I can tell you which one to avoid should you visit Tokyo; although, of course, that one may have improved following her complaint.

We had four presentations lined up over the following three days, all to major international companies, Hitachi, Toyota, National Panasonic and Sony. Once again, we revised our presentation for each, though by then, even Jin-Ae had little heart for going on making new tweaks. Or, more likely, we were both nervous of the risk of getting into another argument.

The first meeting set the scene for all the others. Of all the countries I've been to, Japan is the most culturally unique. It's different in every way. Compared to my previous visit, I noted that a lot more Japanese could speak and understand English, progressing from the near-impossibility of communication in 2000 to quite-difficult-but-possible in 2006. But all the signage in the street, on shops, on transport, was still only in Japanese, unlike in Korea or China. I was concerned that I'd be presenting to people who didn't understand a word, but Jin-Ae assured me that the audience for our meetings were expecting my talk and the slides to be in English, and the people present would understand. Nevertheless, she had added Japanese translations to all the slides.

What can't be translated is the culture, and I wasn't prepared for the different business etiquette. Even having read the book. I'd assumed it would be like Korea, but no.

Just as in Seoul, we made a point of arriving early to get the computer and projector connected before the official start time. Each meeting was scheduled to last exactly one hour, usually beginning at 11am. So, at 10.45 on Monday, we arrived at Hitachi's offices. A secretary escorted us to a meeting room, and we were told to wait, standing. Another young woman arrived; she didn't speak English, but Jin-

Ae translated that she was the Feng Shui consultant. Never met one of those before. Her role was to tell us how the room should be arranged and, specifically, where each of us should sit or stand. We hadn't foreseen this additional step, so it was a rush after that to get set up. I hoped the Feng Shui was good!

On the stroke of 11, a small procession of men – our audience – walked in, stood in line behind the chairs on the opposite side of the conference room table, and bowed. We bowed back. Backs straightened, they then sat. A young man at the end of the line, clearly the youngest, and possibly the only one who spoke English, introduced the others.

Jin-Ae had instructed me that the presentation should last exactly 45 minutes and that then there would be 15 minutes of questions and answers, and that the total meeting time of 60 minutes must not either over-run or under-run under any circumstances. I assumed that she'd got this from a book, and that it was rubbish really, but I'd rehearsed the presentation to last for 45 minutes, so was fine to go along with at least the first part of it. Since in every meeting I'd ever been in, anywhere in the world, follow-up questions either took no time at all or went on way past the normal finish time; I assumed the same would be true in Japan.

I was wrong. I met the 45-minute deadline on the presentation. Unlike almost every other presentation I had ever made, on this occasion I couldn't judge the audience's mood at all. They sat, totally concentrated on the slides, apparently taking it all in but with absolutely no facial expressions at all. Any of them. Maybe they found it interesting, maybe they found it boring, maybe relevant, maybe irrelevant, maybe too serious, maybe too flippant – I wished I knew.

The questions appeared to be pre-rehearsed. The senior people spoke to the young one in Japanese, and he translated. I answered, and he translated back. Another one. Another one. And one more, that I felt needed a longer answer. Only then did I also notice that there was a clock on the wall opposite me, ticking past 11:59. I opened my mouth and began my answer. To my astonishment, mid-sentence, everyone just stood up, bowed, turned to their right and, in line, walked out of the room. Even while I was talking. They weren't being rude. It's just how meetings in Japan work.

I learned my lesson. For the remaining meetings, we arrived 30 minutes before to allow plenty of time for the Feng Shui. I watched the clock, stopped taking questions at 11:58 and aimed to say "Thank you and goodbye" at 11:59:30. The audience still walked out on the dot of 12, but at least I didn't feel embarrassed, nor was I left with my mouth hanging open, halfway through a sentence. All the audiences in the other meetings proved as formal and impossible to read as the first one. So, whilst I felt all the meetings went well, just as in Korea, we never got any business from any of them.

In retrospect, I think I should have put in more effort to following things up, but my gut feeling was that nothing was going to come from any of them even if I did, and there were more promising (or at least easier) fish to catch and fry in the USA and Europe. But I was thoroughly enjoying the experience. It gave me a lot of food for thought on how to improve my presentations and business meetings; it had been a long time, years in fact, since anyone had seriously critiqued the content or the format of my slides, or my style of presentation. Maybe other colleagues were afraid of me, or simply didn't want to tell the boss he should be doing something better or different. A shame: everyone benefits from constructive critics. Jin-Ae might have irritated me more than anyone ever had before (or at least, none that I could recall), but she also did me a lot of good. It just took me a long time before I appreciated this truth. I couldn't have done that trip without her.

During those days in company with Jin-Ae, my irritation was overwhelming. The chemistry between us continued to deteriorate and become ever more acidic, but we kept at it, delivering each meeting with total professionalism, or at least as near to that as we could aspire.

WEEK 3 - DAY 3

WEDNESDAY – MAKING A BREAK FOR THE EXIT

Looking back, the three big meetings in Tokyo, on Monday, Tuesday, and Wednesday mornings, went by in a blur. We were both due to fly back to London on Thursday, though on different flights. But first, we had one more meeting scheduled for Wednesday afternoon. We'd gone back to the hotel after the morning meeting, and were waiting for a taxi, ready to leave again, when Jin-Ae's phone rang. It was her contact cancelling the meeting; something had come up.

Jin-Ae was disappointed; the meeting was with another big and well-known company, but by now I didn't mind; I felt that we'd actually been very lucky to have got through nearly three weeks of travel with no cancellations or rearrangements. I said I'd go to my room and work through my email backlog. Jin-Ae said we should meet up at 5pm; apart from reviewing the meetings of the past few days, she had "things" that she wanted to discuss with me that couldn't wait until we met again in London, as she was going to take a week's holiday before returning to the office. The thought of discussing "things that couldn't wait" filled me with awful dread.

Returning to my room, the first thing I did was to recheck my flight for the next day. For whatever reason, but probably because it was the best value, I was flying Air France via Paris. Looking at their schedule, I noticed that on a few days of the week – Wednesday being one of them – they had a second flight that left late in the evening. Eureka! A brilliant idea had percolated. I called the airline to see if I could change my ticket and get on the evening flight. Yes, if I could get to Narita in time!

I have never packed so quickly. I rushed down to the front desk, and checked out, not regretting for an instant having to pay for the night ahead even though I wouldn't be sleeping there. I wrote a message for Jin-Ae, saying that an emergency had occurred, and I had to leave on the next flight, sealed it in an envelope and asked for it to be delivered to her room – but only after I'd left. The receptionist couldn't understand why I didn't want it sent up immediately and why I didn't want to phone her room. I know it was appalling cowardice and rude, but I didn't want anything to stop me now.

I was going to get a taxi, despite the cost (although Tokyo taxis are not quite as astronomically priced as some guidebooks make out), but the doorman pointed me to a bus labelled "Narita Express" that was right there in front of the hotel, waiting, just as if it knew that I'd be rushing off to the airport and needed it. So, off I went, back to Narita, and on to Paris and then London.

Never have I enjoyed Air France's foie gras and champagne so much.

DENOUEMENT

Back in London, just over a week later, we were having a board meeting, and I recounted part of this story to my colleagues. I was still more than hyper-irritated, and although I hadn't seen her, I knew that Jin-Ae had come back to work that day. I really didn't want to face her. Chicken, I know. Well, any meeting I had with her would have to be rushed, as I was leaving that afternoon for the airport and another trip, this time to Buenos Aires. A colleague, who clearly thought I was exaggerating the story, volunteered to take over her management; I agreed enthusiastically. A small devil chuckled.

I left for Heathrow feeling a real weight lifted from my shoulders. My fellow director who had volunteered was the most skilled sales professional I'd ever known, and I was confident he could make the most of the Korean and Japanese prospects, as well as being a much stricter manager of Jin-Ae, who had been so difficult for me to cope with, and someone who had proved to me that I had so many shortcomings as a manager.

I'd only been gone from the office for about two hours. I'd reached Heathrow, checked in for my flight, and was sitting in the lounge waiting for boarding when my phone rang.

It was my fellow director.

"You're right. She's completely impossible. I've fired her."

OMG. My initial reaction – right up to getting on the plane – was one of euphoria. I felt justified in having found her impossible to work with. It no longer felt like it was all my fault. Someone else had done something I was too weak to have done myself – though should have.

That feeling didn't last long. When I woke up, on the approach to Ezeiza airport in Buenos Aires, the realisation hit me that if we were to go ahead with the Chinese operation, never mind if we wanted to pursue the sales opportunities in Korea and Japan, we'd need to find a new Jin-Ae, or at least someone with an equal of her language skills. She was going to be a hard act to follow.

Later the same day, somewhat refreshed from my long flight and wandering the streets of my favourite city, my mobile rang. Jin-Ae. In hysterics.

"Please have me back! I will be a good and obedient girl, I promise!"

Well, a lot more than that, but those particular words stay with me, and the rest of the long outburst was much of the same. Contrition was the theme. If she'd waited a day or two, and been calm, quiet and professional, I'm sure I'd have said yes. I may well have been crucified by my fellow directors for doing so, but I think I would have relented. Unfortunately for her, she once again got her timing wrong. After a 15-hour journey, not enough sleep, a little jetlag and getting the call literally while walking down a busy street in the centre of Buenos Aires, it was more than I could take. I said no, no, no, no… a lot of times. And eventually, just to terminate the conversation, hung up on her.

We did go ahead with the Chinese operation, but without Jin-Ae or a replacement. Despite that, it worked fairly well for the next seven or eight years. It never realised every ambition we had for it, though, and managing the enterprise became progressively more difficult. Eventually it was closed down by the company that bought us out. The hard-fought-for prospects in Korea and Japan were never followed up, and never generated any business. Maybe if I'd been able to compromise and find a peaceful working relationship with Jin-Ae, all those things would have flowered to success – but who knows?

Now, the legacy is just that memorable business trip.

Three weeks of hell?

No, three weeks of a very unusual and worthwhile experience, albeit tinged with huge dollops of frustration.

There really is 'no business like international business'!

*

WHATEVER HAPPENED TO JIN-AE?

Poor Jin-Ae.

Abandoned by me in Japan, sacked, then begging for her job back and my hanging up on her…

Don't think I didn't have regrets. Still do. She drove me crazy over those three weeks, but she had definitely done her job, and done it very well too.

I over-reacted.

Frankly, she was quite right about being worth more than Greta or Hannah, at least when she was being calm and professional; if she hadn't insisted on arguing about her salary in the middle of the street in Shanghai and Seoul, I've little doubt that she'd have been paid what she asked for, that we'd have continued to work together and that our business would have prospered more than it did. Certainly, our project with Donald would have worked out better; for a decade after that, I missed her every time I visited Shanghai.

I hope that she went on to better and more interesting things. That she secured work where she could apply all her talents and where they would be properly appreciated. With more tolerant colleagues, or at least in an environment where she could keep the more obstreperous side of her personality in check more of the time.

She made a lasting and significant impact on me. Which is part of the reason, I suppose, for my immortalising her here in print. She made our trip together to Asia a stand-out; more memorable than hundreds of others I have undertaken.

And – I never think I've seen quite the last of her.

Somehow, I'm still expecting her to resurface… and tell me how to do my life better. Older, and more tolerant, if not necessarily wiser for the years that have elapsed in between, I might be more inclined to listen to her… but, then again, I might not!

EPILOGUE

It may strike you as odd to write about business trips now, when international travel is beset by a host of complications – PCR tests, quarantines, government approval documents, even vaccination passports. I didn't intend it as a sentimental recollection along the lines of "wish I was back there" (though often I do).

Environmentalists present persuasive argument for why we should curtail business travel. They have a point, and it's easy to find examples of unnecessary journeys, especially now we live in a world of Zoom, Teams, Google Meets, Skype and a host of online platforms. However, I don't believe that most business travellers choose to get on a plane as an excuse for a "jolly" somewhere sunny, or just to get away from the office. The underlying purpose of almost all such trips is to nurture the growth of international trade, to meet people face to face, and look each other in the eyes.

Certainly, that's why I made the journeys I describe in this book.

I couldn't have substituted video conferencing for any part of them – and I travelled not only in the full knowledge of its existence (indeed, I was very much an "early adopter"), but as the leader of a company dedicated to helping its clients reduce their energy usage and improving the environment. Essential business travel will have to resume. It will be interesting to see how much impact the environmental lobby will have once the pandemic complications have become 'normal' and manageable.

There has also been a growing backlash against 'globalisation', pushed to the fore by Trump, but echoed by would-be dictators in other countries, and simple nationalism in many others. But no single country can be self-sufficient – or at least, cannot on its own maintain the style of living that its population has come to enjoy and expect. Surely, also, in the pursuit of peace, happiness and economic success for all countries, we should each of us embrace the world's different cultures, and aim to get closer rather than farther apart?

That's the spirit in which I've made all my international travel, whether for business or pleasure (and, where possible, both).